British Buses and Trolleybuses 1950s-1970s

British Buses and Trolleybuses
1950s-1970s

The operators and their vehicles
Part 2: South Wales
Henry Conn

CRUMLIN

GWO 351C

SLP Silver Link Publishing Ltd

First published in 2010

British Library Cataloguing in Publication Data

A catalogue record for this book is available from the British Library.

ISBN 978 1 85794 342 9

Silver Link Publishing Ltd
The Trundle
Ringstead Road
Great Addington
Kettering
Northants NN14 4BW

Tel/Fax: 01536 330588
email: sales@nostalgiacollection.com
Website: www.nostalgiacollection.com

Printed and bound in the Czech Republic

All photographs were taken by the author or are from his collection unless otherwise credited. Those labelled 'transporttreasury. co.uk' are obtainable from Transport Treasury.

Title page: **In 1974 West Monmouthshire Omnibus Board became Islwyn Borough Transport, and with that came a change of livery. The new livery is worn by No 17 (GWO 351C), and this view can be contrasted with the earlier picture of the same bus in West Mon livery on page 121. This wonderful shot was taken on 20 May 1978 at Cwmsyfiog.** *Geoff Gould*

Acknowledgements

Most of the photographs within this book have come from my archive, but very special thanks are due to David Clarke for his wonderful portraits of and Cardiff trolleybuses, to Geoff Gould for access to his superb collection of photographs of South Wales buses and for his very much appreciated time and thoughts, and to the Transport Treasury, where some of my archive of photographs are kept. Finally, many, many thanks to the team at Silver Link Publishing who agreed to publish this book.

The PSV Circle publications of all the operators illustrated in this book were vital sources of information.

Contents

Introduction 7

Aberdare Urban District Council (Cynon Valley) 9

Bedwas & Machen Urban District Council 12

Brewer's 16

Caerphilly Urban District Council 18

Cardiff Corporation 24

R. I. Davies & Son 38

O. J. Edwards & Sons 40

Eltys Motors 42

Eynon's 43

Gelligaer Urban District Council 46

Henley's 50

Jones (Aberbeeg) 52

David Jones (Abergwilli) 56

Llynfi Motors 58

Merthyr Tydfil Corporation 62

Newport Corporation 66

Peakes 70

Pontypridd Urban District Council 73

Porthcawl Omnibus 80

Red & White Services 83

Rees & Williams 87

Richards Brothers 91

Rhondda Transport Co 93

Silcox Motor Coach Co 98

South Wales Transport Co 100

Thomas Brothers 111

Tudor Williams 114

United Welsh Services 115

West Monmouthshire Omnibus Board (Islwyn) 117

West Wales 122

Western Welsh Omnibus Co 126

Above: In the low sunshine of early April in Castle Street, Cardiff, is No 286 (KBO 959). In this busy scene the first two cars turning right are both Austin/Morris 1100s. The car behind the trolleybus is a Morris Minor and the bus coming towards the camera is a Guy Arab. *David Clarke*

Below: This view of Willowbrook-bodied AEC Reliance No 33 (JTX 233D), new to Aberdare in June 1966, was taken at Gadlys on 4 July 1977. Just behind is a Rover SD1, although the car was never marketed as such – most of us know it as the Rover 3500. The initial May 1976 launch was for the 3500 only, but a little over a year later the 2300 and 2600 were added. The SD1 was popular with the police in this country, particularly the V8 model. Between 1976 and 1986 just over 300,000 of the various models of the SD1 were produced. *Geoff Gould*

Introduction

This is the second volume in the series, this time taking a nostalgic look at buses and trolleybuses in South Wales, with illustrations taken from the late 1950s through to the mid-1970s. As in the Midlands volume, I have included all the main bus operators in the area, but in addition there are numerous independent bus operators, many of which purchased buses from the larger operators near their field of operations.

The bulk of buses in Wales were to be found in the densely populated industrial south. The largest municipal operator was Cardiff Corporation, which in 1961 had a fleet size of 258, which included 79 trolleybuses. The traditional livery was crimson and cream, but a new orange livery was adopted during 1972. A joint service was operated by Cardiff and Newport Corporations between the two cities. In 1961 Newport had a fleet of 121 buses, of which 15 were single-deck. By the early 1970s the last Leyland Titans had been withdrawn and the oldest buses in the fleet were 1966 Alexander-bodied Leyland Atlanteans. During 1971 Newport began converting its buses to one-person operation and took delivery, over two years, of 44 Metro-Scania dual-doorway buses. Later, Newport also purchased some redundant Metro-Scanias from London Transport, thus giving the city the honour of having the biggest fleet in the UK of this relatively short-lived bus.

The other South Wales municipal fleets were based in the valleys. West Monmouthshire Omnibus Board, based in Blackwood in the mid-1960s, had a fleet strength of 30 buses, most of which were Leylands. Caerphilly Urban District

Below: **Caerphilly purchased two Massey-bodied Leyland PSU3/1Rs in October 1964, Nos 14 and 15 (ATX 514B and 515B). Seen at Caerphilly station in April 1970 is No 15.** *Geoff Gould*

Council, in the Rhymney Valley, had 31 buses in a green and cream livery. Gelligaer UDC had a similar number of buses with a livery of red, white and green, and Bedwas & Machen had a 1961 fleet of seven buses with a dark blue and cream livery. The Rhymney Valley District Council took over the three fleets in 1974 and introduced a new and distinctive livery of brown, yellow and cream.

Pontypridd, during the mid-1960s, had a fleet strength of around 50 buses, the majority of which were of AEC manufacture. The fleet livery at that time was dark blue and cream, but this was changed in 1971 to light blue and cream. Pontypridd had the distinction of having the last two half-cab double-deckers, a pair of AEC Regent Vs, supplied to a Welsh bus operator. To the north, Merthyr Tydfil had an uninspiring maroon and cream livery and in the early 1960s had a fleet strength of 76 buses, of which ten were single-deck. From 1966, however, through to the mid-1970s, Merthyr only purchased single-deck buses. Aberdare, with its also uninspiring all-over maroon livery, still had a few Guy Arabs in service in the early 1970s, but by 1975 the fleet was made up of 19 AEC Reliance's and six AEC Swifts.

The headquarters of Red & White was in Chepstow and its operations extended to Swansea, Brecon, Newport, Cardiff, and across the border to Gloucester and Hereford. The fleet was made up almost entirely of Bristols. Western Welsh, whose main works were situated at Ely, Cardiff, operated services throughout a considerable part of South Wales. Western Welsh had quite a varied fleet of buses that included very early Weymann lowbridge-bodied Leyland Atlanteans, together with Leyland Titans, Regents and Renowns. The single-deckers were Marshall- or Weymann-bodied Leyland Tiger Cubs and Leopards. Rhondda Transport had a similar fleet to Western Welsh.

Jones of Aberbeeg was an independent operator until 1969 when it was sold to the National Bus Company. At that time it operated 43 buses, which ran in the Jones livery of blue and white until 1975. South Wales Transport, with its main workshops at Ravenhill in Swansea, operated a large fleet, most of which were of AEC manufacture. This fleet was increased to around 500 buses in 1971 when the fleets of United Welsh, Thomas Brothers and Neath & Cardiff were taken over.

There were a large number of well established independent operators in South Wales. At Abertillery, Henley's ran two local services. Several services in the Pontypool area were run by Peakes. At Maesteg, Brewer of Caerau operated services using buses purchased new. From Maesteg to Port Talbot a service was provided by Llynfi Motor Services, run jointly with South Wales Transport, and extended to Aberavon Beach. Seen regularly on this service was Llynfi's 1958 Massey-bodied Leyland Titan. West Wales was a company based at Tycroes and had purchased, new, an AEC Renown. However, by the mid-1970s the fleet was made up almost exclusively of Leylands, most of which were Leopards. Also based in Tycroes was Rees & Williams, which ran Leopards on services from Llandeilo to Swansea and Llanelli. Eynon of Trimsaran ran a service from Llanelli to Carmarthen, and Thomas Brothers of Llangadog operated a Llandeilo to Carmarthen service. The area around Pembroke and Tenby was served by one of the biggest Welsh independents, Silcox Motor Coach Company, which at times operated a fleet in excess of 60 buses, many of which were second-hand Bristols. Richard Brothers had a substantial network of services in the Haverfordwest, Fishguard and Cardigan areas.

Enjoy the nostalgia!

Aberdare Urban District Council (Cynon Valley)

Aberdare was one of only eight post-war Urban District Council undertakings and ran services in or around the Cynon Valley in Glamorgan. Trams were first operated by the Council in 1913, and by 1922 5¾ miles of track were operated. Aberdare also operated trolleybuses from 1914, but during 1921 and 1922 the trolleybus operations ceased, and for a short time Tilling Stevens buses were used. These buses were then used to start a network of bus routes in the early 1920s. From 1925 to 1933 Bristol buses were purchased, followed by Daimlers, and the first double-decker was an AEC Regent. The tramways ceased in 1935. Just after the war a fleet of Bristols were acquired, following which the fleet had deliveries of Guy Arabs, AEC Regents and AEC Reliances.

Above: **Originally, the Aberdare livery was maroon with cream relief, but by the 1960s this had changed to cream with bands of a pale red. Seen in August 1972 in this livery is No 58 (XNY 414), one of a batch of five Longwell Green-bodied Guy Arab IVs new to Aberdare in 1958. I think Longwell Green Coachworks was in some way descended from one of the Bence businesses. The Bence family were** wheelwrights at Longwell Green, near Bristol, **and in the late 1960s the firm was making bodywork on various lorry chassis, and had been a builder of bus bodies. Its products had been especially popular with bus operators in South Wales. Longwell Green Coachworks was situated along the south side of Kingfield Lane at its junction with Bath Road.** *Geoff Gould*

Above: The Swift was AEC's offering for the late-1960s rear-engined bandwagon. In fact it was designed after the takeover of AEC by Leyland and was little more than a Leyland Panther with AEC mechanical parts. It also suffered some of the shortcomings of its much-unloved Leyland counterpart, but its reliability wasn't quite so bad and it outlasted the Panther by a number of years, even continuing in production for a couple of years after the Leyland National was introduced. It came in 33- and 36-foot lengths, but London Transport chose to apply the name Merlin to its 36-foot models. I think the uniform of the driver is great, and I presume from his dress that July 1977 must have been hot. No 11 (FNY 991K) was one of six Willowbrook AEC Swifts delivered in 1971. *Geoff Gould*

Opposite top: In 1912 the London General Omnibus Company was taken over by the Underground group of companies, which at that time owned most of the London Underground and extensive tram operations. As part of the reorganisation following the takeover, a separate concern was set up for the bus manufacturing elements, and was named Associated Equipment Company, or more commonly AEC. AEC's first commercial vehicle was a lorry based on the X-Type bus chassis. With the outbreak of war in 1914, AEC's ability to produce large numbers of vehicles using assembly line methods became important in supplying the increasing need for army lorries. The company began large-scale production of the 3-ton Y-Type lorry in 1916 and continued beyond the end of the war. From then on AEC became associated with both lorries and buses. Seen at Cwmdare in August 1972 is No 34 (JTX 234D), the last of a batch of six Willowbrook-bodied dual-door AEC Reliances, which were new to Aberdare in June 1966. *Geoff Gould*

Below: **Three ECW Bristol RESL6Ls, Nos 42 to 44, were delivered to Cynon Valley in May 1975. Seen in Cwmaman is No 42, (HTG 353N). The Ford Corsair, gleaming in the sunshine, was a medium-sized car available as either a saloon or an estate from 1964 until 1970. It was designed around a lengthened Cortina Mark 1 floor pan,** and shared many of its mechanical and body components with the Cortina. The Corsair had unusual and quite bold styling for its day, with a sharp horizontal V-shaped crease at the very front of the car into which round headlights were inset. Between 1964 and 1970 more than 310,000 Corsairs were produced. *Geoff Gould*

Bedwas & Machen Urban District Council

Bedwas & Machen Council obtained powers to operate buses in 1917 and a service to Caerphilly was started. For a long time the fleet consisted of only three buses and was the smallest municipal fleet in the country. Until 1947 no double-deckers were owned, but in that year two 17-year-old Leyland TD1s were acquired from Wigan Corporation. Albion Venturers with Welsh Metal Industries bodywork were purchased in 1948, but for many years subsequently AEC buses were acquired.

Right: **Bedwas & Machen was an urban district in the county of Monmouthshire from 1912 to 1974, and was one of the smallest municipal bus undertakings in the UK with an average fleet size of seven vehicles. The bus livery was blue and cream, and representative of** this smart livery is No 5 (422 CAX), a Massey lowbridge-bodied AEC Regent V delivered in December 1961. The fleet was merged with that of Caerphilly and Gelligaer UDCs in April 1974, when Rhymney Valley District Council was formed.

Left: **Delivered in August 1964 was another Massey lowbridge-bodied AEC Regent V, No 8 (BWO 585B). This photograph was taken on 23 March 1974, just a few days before the merger with Rhymney District Council.** *Geoff Gould*

Above: This is Caerphilly bus station, adjacent to the railway station, in March 1974. About to depart for Newport is No 10 (OAX 74M), one of two Leyland PSU3B/2Rs with East Lancashire bodywork that were delivered in 1973. The pair were the last buses to enter service with the UDC, before the merger into the Rhymney District Council. *Geoff Gould*

Right: In Caerphilly in October 1973, heading for Newport, is No 9, (GAX 423L), a Willowbrook-bodied Leyland PSU3B/2R delivered in November 1972. *Geoff Gould*

Brewer's

Brothers A. E. and F. R. Brewer were farmers who gave their neighbours lifts in their farm vehicles and decided, in 1920, to regularise this arrangement by starting a timetabled bus service. This ran the short distance from the mining village of Caerau into the local town of Maesteg along the Llynfi valley, and the routes between the two places remained the basis of Brewer's bus operations throughout the company's existence. Both of these views of Brewer's buses were taken in 1964 at the Maesteg terminus, behind the Town Hall, which was used by all operators, and both buses are on the Caerau route.

Below: **The first view is of GTX 162, an AEC Regal originally coach-bodied by Duple, but re-bodied by Neath Coachworks in 1959, remaining in service until 1968. There were (and still are) two parallel routes between Maesteg and Caerau via either Tonna Road (the 'top road') or via Coegnant Road, which runs along the bottom of the valley. Brewer's also operated services to other parts of Maesteg but no regular long-distance routes.**

Above: (OTG 601), a Weymann-bodied AEC Reliance purchased new by Brewer's in 1954, has apparently had a little argument with something solid. The bus was sold to South Wales Transport in January 1988, a sale prompted, I think, by the desire of Mrs Watts, the then manager and surviving active member of the Brewer family, to retire; I assume that there were no further heirs, or at least none interested in continuing the business. SWT kept the Brewer's name and operations separate, I suspect because Brewer's staff were employed on more flexible working conditions than applied in SWT. The Brewer's unit was used to both acquire other bus operations in the area, for example Llynfi Motors of Maesteg, six months later in July 1988, Burrows of Ogmore Vale in October 1993 and Porthcawl Omnibus Company in October 1996, and also for SWT's expansion into the Bridgend area when National Welsh went into receivership in January 1992. Within days in that same month (January 1992) Brewer's strengthened its position in Bridgend by taking over the local town routes provided by Morris Travel of Pencoed, some of which Morris had earlier acquired from Coity Motors. SWT became part of Badgerline in February 1990, and thus part of First Bus (later First Group) in June 1995. Both the Brewer's and SWT operations were renamed First Cymru from 1 April 1998.

Caerphilly Urban District Council

This small Glamorgan municipal fleet gained powers to operate buses in 1917. From that time a number of inter-urban routes were developed, including a 33-mile route between Cardiff and Tredegar. Early buses used were Tilling Stevens, but between 1930 and 1940 Thornycroft, Dennis and Daimler single-deck buses were purchased. The first double-deck buses operated were two utility Daimler CWA6s, delivered in 1943. The following year saw the purchase from Wolverhampton Corporation of some Daimlers and Guys, all of which had utility bodies. In 1947 four Fodens were purchased, followed by a number of Guy Arab IIs in 1948 and 1949. From the early 1950s Leylands were purchased.

Opposite top: **Leyland introduced a separate underfloor-engined chassis, suitable for the range of bodywork preferred by many of its customers. It was named 'Royal Tiger' and designated PSU1, the 'U' signifying an underfloor engine. Eight models were offered for the domestic market, designated PSU1/9 to PSU1/16, all with a 15ft 7in wheelbase and an overall width of either 7ft 6in (PSU1/9-12) or 8 feet (PSU1/13-16). The designations PSU1/1 to PSU1/8 were never built, since they were intended to be 27ft 6in long; amendments to the Construction & Use Regulations made them obsolete before they could be built. The first production Royal Tiger buses were three for Ramsbottom UDC in 1950, and it became an instant success, especially abroad, were the model was ordered in great numbers. This April 1970 view is of Caerphilly No 9 (UTX 9), a Massey-bodied Leyland PSU1/13 delivered in May 1956.** *Geoff Gould*

Right: **On 1 April 1974, under Government reorganisation, Caerphilly Urban District Council became part of the Rhymney Valley District Council. The Caerphilly fleet was merged with the fleets of Gelligaer and Bedwas & Machen to form the new Rhymney Valley District Council fleet. The Rhymney Valley livery in 1979 was, dare I say it, interesting to say the least. This excellent view of No 34 (GTX 734C), the last of the Massey-bodied Leyland PD3/4s delivered in late 1965, was taken at Markham on 2 July 1979.** *Geoff Gould*

Above: **In November 1972 Caerphilly purchased two Willowbrook-bodied Leyland PSU3B/2Rs, Nos 4 and 5 (KNY 924L and 925L), and seen at Caerphilly railway station on 29 March 1975 is No 4. It is still wearing CUDC green but has the Rhymney Valley fleet name just below the first window.** *Geoff Gould*

Below: **Two Leyland PD3/4s, Nos 29 and 30, (557 MNY and 558 MNY), with Massey lowbridge bodywork, were delivered in November 1961, and seen here is No 29. The Leyland PD3/4 model had synchromesh transmission, air brakes and** an exposed radiator. **Parked to the front of No 29 is a Ford Prefect, and in the background are a Mini and a Ford Anglia.** *Geoff Gould*

Opposite top: **Caerphilly took delivery of three Massey-bodied Leyland PD3/4s between October and December 1965, Nos 32 to 34 (GNY 432C, GNY 433C and GTX 734C). This view of No 32 (GNY 432C) was taken at Caerphilly station on 29 March 1975 with the bus still in CUDC livery, but with the Rhymney Valley fleet name.** *Geoff Gould*

Below: Two Massey lowbridge-bodied Leyland PD2/37s arrived in October 1966, and seen here is the second of them, No 36 (LNY 536D). Seating upstairs was four-abreast with a sunken gangway at the offside, presenting a grave hazard to the heads of forgetful passengers rising from their seats in the lower saloon! It also gave the vehicles a rather dumpy appearance. The cab is ventilated by an unusual hinged window instead of the customary sliding panel. This bus is now in preservation with the Rhymney Valley Transport Preservation Society. *Geoff Gould*

Inset opposite: **Caerphilly was a keen purchaser of Leyland PD3/4s with Massey bodywork, and No 31 (31 SNY), new in March 1963, is seen here in the livery of Rhymney Valley District Council in Markham on 22 September 1978.** *Geoff Gould*

Main picture: **Two more Leyland PD2/37s, Nos 37 and 38 (ONY 637F and ONY 638F), with Massey 64-seat front-entrance bodies, arrived in December 1967. This excellent view of No 38 was taken near Tredegar in July 1972. After the delivery of these buses, only 15 more Leyland PD2s were built, of which nine were delivered to Wigan between March and May 1968, and six to Darwen, three in April 1968 and three in April 1969. In my opinion, Nos 37 and 38 were not the most elegant-looking of buses.** *Geoff Gould*

Cardiff Corporation

Cardiff Corporation commenced tram operations in 1902 and the system that was built up remained intact until 1942, when one route was converted to trolleybuses. In 1946 the Corporation ordered more trolleybuses, and on 19 February 1950 tram operations ceased. The 1941 trolleybuses were AEC 664Ts, but all post-war trolleybuses are BUT 9641Ts, three-axle models with East Lancashire bodywork. The 1955 trolleybuses replaced buses on the Ely route, and the system remained unchanged until 25 November 1962 when route 2 was converted to bus operation. The first buses owned were single- and double-deck petrol/electric Tilling Stevens. Between 1928 and 1931 Albion, Bristol, Dennis and Thornycroft buses were acquired. In 1932 Leyland Tigers and Titans were delivered, but in the following year AEC Regents were purchased, and for the next few years AEC buses were regularly delivered. During the war Bristols, Guys and Bedfords were allocated to Cardiff. Immediately after the war AEC buses returned, together with Daimler CVD6s, Crossley DD42s and some Bruce-bodied Bristol KSW6Gs. During the 1950s Guy Arab and Daimler double-deckers were purchased, together with Leyland single-deckers.

Opposite: **Cardiff was quite late in introducing trolleybuses, the first examples taking to the streets on 1 March 1942, when trolleybuses replaced trams on the route between Wood Street and Clarence Road. The intention had been to replace the city's remaining trams with trolleybuses in 1939, but the outbreak of war delayed matters. Ten AEC 664T trolleybuses with Bruce bodywork had been purchased, being the last of that chassis manufactured by AEC. Of the ten, only five entered service immediately, the other five being delivered later in the year. All ten entered service in a drab wartime grey livery. However, in 1946 at least four of these vehicles were repainted in a streamlined crimson lake and cream livery; the others remained in grey until, by 1949/50, all ten had all been repainted in standard motorbus livery. This is Cowbridge Road East on 1 April 1969, and No 215 (DBO 475) is working on route 10. There is a fine selection of cars in view, the nearest being a very clean-looking Morris Minor. Running behind No 215 is a Mini and, I think, a Hillman Hunter. Just emerging from the Esso service station is a Hillman Imp.** *David Clarke*

Above: **The trolleybus system expanded until the last extension (to Ely) was inaugurated in May 1955, taking the trolleybus fleet strength to 79 vehicles, of which six were single-deckers for use on the Pier Head via Bute Street service. The busiest trolleybus route in Cardiff served the large Ely housing estate. The services were provided in the form of a loop running out via Cowbridge Road and returning via Grand Avenue, or vice versa. The main service operated along Macdonald Road, which can be seen diverging to the left from Grand Avenue at this point. The trolleybus in the picture has come from Green Farm Road; this was an extra loop served in one direction only, by about one in three of the journeys operating clockwise. Seen here in 1966 is No 228 (DUH 723), one of 20 BUT 9641Ts with East Lancashire bodywork delivered in 1948. All the early batches of 9641Ts were delivered with front entrances and rear exits for pay-as-you-enter operation, but were all later converted to rear entrance only.**

Above: This is Cardiff Central Bus Station, which was opened in the 1950s and still functions in much the same way as in this view taken in 1968, with buses following an anti-clockwise movement to park in parallel rows of bays. The bus station has been remodelled (more than once), and the rows are now much straighter than the curved layout shown, and the separate small shelters were replaced by a continuous covered walkway along each row. The bus is No 29 (GUH 934), one of 20, Nos 26 to 40 (GUH 931 to 945), which were D. J. Davies-bodied Guy Arab IIIs, delivered during 1953. Glengettie is a blend of tea aimed at Welsh consumers and was first marketed in 1952 as a stronger brew, blended for Welsh miners, but today the focus is on the strength in flavour and its qualities as a 'premium' tea. The packaging is unusual in that it is bilingual, English and Welsh, with opposite sides of the box carrying text in each language. The Glengettie range is available from leading supermarkets and grocers, predominantly in Wales and surrounding areas. *Geoff Gould*

Above: In November 1961 the decision was taken by the City Council to convert all trolleybus services to motorbus operation over a period of eight to ten years. The first to go was the Pengam and St Mary Street service in November 1962. Conversions to motorbus continued at regular intervals until the last trolleybuses were withdrawn on 11 January 1970, when the 10A and 10B Ely service was finally converted to motorbus operation. The last new trolleybuses for Cardiff Corporation were delivered during 1955, and numerically the first was No 275 (KBO 948), seen here on Grand Avenue in April 1969. The car parked on the pavement is a Ford Anglia. *David Clarke*

Above: Travelling along Westgate Street in early April 1969 are, nearest the camera, No 283 (KBO 956), and, in the distance, No 276 (KBO 949). The white car parked on the opposite side of the road is a Hillman Hunter, which was first produced in 1966. This particular car was registered in 1969. *David Clarke*

Below: **At the beginning of 1969 there were only four trolleybus systems still operating – Bradford, Teesside, Walsall and Cardiff. This view of No 277 (KBO 950) was taken on Grand Avenue on what looks to be a lovely early spring day in April 1969. Grand Avenue links Cowbridge Road West to the northern estates of Ely. The Ely estate was very much influenced by the Garden City movement, and was based around a wide tree-lined avenue called Grand Avenue, which stretches for more than a mile across the suburb. At one time the estate was the largest municipal housing provided in Europe, and families moved here from the crowded streets of Splott, Adamsdown and Butetown.** *David Clarke*

Above: **Twelve East Lancashire-bodied Guy Arab IVs, Nos 343 to 354 (OUH 343 to 354), arrived in 1958, and seen in Cardiff Bus Station in 1968 is one of that batch, No 345 (OUH 345). In 1950 Guy presented the Arab IV, and Lancashire United was the first to purchase the model, complete with Weymann H57R bodies. At first designed to meet the needs of Birmingham City Transport, the Arab IV came with a 27-foot-long body and a 16ft 4in wheelbase, available in 7ft 6in or 8ft 0in widths. During 1956 a 30-foot-long chassis with an 18ft 6in wheelbase was introduced, when the law allowed it. Guy Arab IVs received power from a variety of engines, the Gardner 5LW and 6LW and Meadows 10.35-litre 6DC630. The brakes were either of the vacuum-aided triple-servo variety or air brakes, as, for example, with the 30-foot chassis. There was some overlap in production of Mark III and IV Arabs until 1953, in which year an exposed radiator was available for Mark IV buses for those customers who favoured that version. Production of the Arab IV was discontinued in 1960, although some buses were built in 1962, but by then the Wulfrunian and Arab Mark V were available to operators.** *Geoff Gould*

Below: **This is No 283 (KBO 956) on Cowbridge Road West in early April 1969.** *David Clarke*

Numerically the last of the trolleybuses received by Cardiff was No 287 (KBO 960), seen here passing No 282 (KBO 955) at Victoria Park in early April 1969. Victoria Park, which covers nearly 20 acres, was created as a municipal recreation ground by Cardiff City Council through a city charter between 1897 and 1898 to celebrate Queen Victoria's Diamond Jubilee.

It was the first municipal park established within Cardiff, and was one of the first in the country. The car disappearing between the two trolleybuses is a 1968 Ford Cortina Mark II.

The trolleybuses ceased to operate in Cardiff in January 1970. *David Clarke*

Above: **Seen in Gabalfa during March 1973 is the first of a batch of ten Leyland PD2A/20s with East Lancashire bodies, Nos 392 to 401 (392 to 401 BUH), which were new in February 1963. I believe that Kardov self-raising flour was produced in both Cardiff and Swansea. The Vauxhall HA van, an example of which is seen on the right, was eventually supplanted by the Chevanne. However, due to fleet orders, particularly from British Telecom and the Post Office, the HA van actually stayed in production** using the later HC Viva's engine, gearbox and rear axle, until 1983. The rather elderly Hillman Minx, which I think is a Series III, dates from around the late 1950s/early 1960s, and seems to be taking a rather dodgy route round the parked cars. *Geoff Gould*

Below: **In late 1963 and early 1964 Cardiff Corporation received 12 AEC Regent Vs. The first six, Nos 408 to 413 (408 to 413 DBO), were bodied by East Lancashire, while the remainder, Nos 414 to 419 (414 to 419 DBO), had their frames made by East Lancashire, but were completed by Neepsend. Neepsend was associated with East Lancashire coachbuilders and its works were at Penistone Road in Sheffield. In Cardiff Bus Station in February 1974 is No 414 (414 DBO).** *Geoff Gould*

Above: **This is No 412 (412 DBO) at Victoria Park on 27 July 1976, one of a batch of 12 AEC Regent Vs that arrived in late 1963 and early 1964, and one of six that had East Lancashire bodywork. If you look closely, both cars behind the bus are Morris Marinas. The half-obscured one can be identified, because of its grille, as a Morris Marina 1.3-litre two-door coupé, and the other is the more 'sporty' Marina 1.8TC.** *Geoff Gould*

Right: **During 1968 Cardiff received 20 Alexander W-Type dual-door-bodied AEC Swifts. They were numbered 506 to 525 (MBO 506F to 525F), and at the junction of High Street and Duke Street in February 1974 is No 518 (MBO 518F).** *Geoff Gould*

Opposite top: **By 1939 Guy was very much on the sidelines of bus-making, but the war saved the bus production side of the company. During the war Guy was permitted to build utility double-decker vehicles based on the pre-war Arab and Vix-Ant lorries, getting the business mainly because it had spare bus manufacturing capacity. War-time double-deck production was shared approximately equally between Guy and Daimler, and many single-deck buses were built by Bedford, all under Government sanction. Guy produced very large numbers of these Arab buses during the war years; proving to be very reliable, they formed the basis of Guy's post-war reputation as a bus-maker. Many operators that had Arabs 'inflicted' on them by the Ministry of Supply during the war went on to buy Guy vehicles from choice for**

many years after. Thirty-seven Guy Arab Vs were delivered to Cardiff Corporation in 1966 and all were bodied by Alexander; this one, No 441 (EUH 441D), has travelled along South Mary Street and turned west into Wood Street in this 1968 view. The bus has only a few yards to go to reach the Central Bus Station. Boots chemist shop on the right still exists, but the other shops visible have changed hands. Brains Brewery in central Cardiff, with the chimney visible in the background, has been demolished, and the area is now a courtyard of restaurants and café bars with flats above, called the Brewery Quarter. *transporttreasury.co.uk*

R. I. Davies & Son

R. I. Davies of Tredegar and Merthyr Council had shared the route from Merthyr Tydfil the few miles northwards as far as Cefn-coed-y-cymmer, which is in effect the last sizeable community that can be considered part of Merthyr before the road to Brecon continues into the more rugged southern slopes of the Brecon Beacons. But beyond Cefn-coed-y-cymmer and off to the right is the housing estate of Trefechan, and beyond that the village of Pontsticill. Both were served solely by Davies until Merthyr Tydfil Council took over that route in March 1976.

Above: **Working on the Merthyr to Trefechan route during July 1972 is (879 DTB), a Guy Arab IV with Northern Counties bodywork. This bus was new to Lancashire United as its No 612 in 1958 and was withdrawn in early 1972.**

Left: **Also working the Merthyr to Trefechan route for R. I. Davies on the same July day is (LFS 409), a Metro-Cammell-bodied Leyland PD2/20 new to Edinburgh Corporation as its No 409 in 1954. Edinburgh's buses were still outnumbered by trams until 1952. Between 1953 and 1957 Edinburgh Corporation received 370 new buses and a further 77 were overhauled and rebodied. No 409 was one of a batch of 100 PD2/20s delivered during 1954 and many of the earlier-delivered buses of this batch replaced trams on the Corstorphine routes during March 1954.** *Geoff Gould*

O. J. Edwards & Sons

Vauxhall Motors introduced the Bedford OB in 1939 as a replacement for the WTB and, like the WTB, it was powered by a six-cylinder petrol engine of 3519cc, also known as the 28hp unit. Where the OB differed from its predecessor

was with the chassis, specially designed for PSV use; previously an adapted lorry chassis had been used. The OB chassis has an offset differential in the rear axle with the engine and four-speed sliding mesh (crash) gearbox mounted at a slight angle to enable the propeller shaft to line up with the differential, which was set to the near side of the axle. This enabled a sunken gangway to be installed along the centre line of the coach. Production commenced in 1939, but with the outbreak of war only

73 had been built, with 52 going to the UK market before hostilities halted production later that year. In 1942, in line with strict Ministry of Supply specifications, production recommenced on a wartime austerity version, the OWB, one of the few Government-approved chassis sanctioned for wartime production. The 29- or 32-seat bus bodies were in the main built by Duple and Roe, to a standard design that included wooden slatted seats. When the war ended in 1945 production of the OWB ceased after some 3,300 had been built, and production of the OB recommenced. Many OWBs soldiered on in service until the early 1950s, when a number were rebodied with the Duple Vista coach body, new chassis being in short supply and on a long waiting list. Between 1939 and 1951 Bedford produced a total of 16,164 OB and OWB chassis, the majority of which were bodied by Duple Vista with either 27- or 29-seat coach bodies. Forty-six other manufacturers, including Plaxton, Mulliner, SMT and Thurgood, produced bodies for the OB, which in the main were of a similar design to Duple.

Working a schools service in Crymmych in May 1973 is an ex-Ministry of Defence Almet-bodied Bedford OB, (JXX 487), belonging to O. J. Edwards & Sons of Maenclochog.

Eltys Motors

In September 1973 the Edwards business (see previous page) passed to E. J. Lewis and T. L. Jenkins, who traded as Eltys Motors of Maenclochog, and introduced a blue livery.

Seen here is another of Edwards's ex-Ministry of Defence Bedford OBs, (JXX 461), also bodied by Almet, leaving Crymmych School in June 1979. Just behind is another of Eltys buses, (FYC 127C), a Willowbrook-bodied Bedford VAM5 new to Wakes of Sparkford, Somerset, in December 1965. Noteworthy is the fact that in 1998 there were still three ex-Ministry of Defence Bedford OBs on Eltys Motors' premises.

Eynon's

Samuel Eynon worked at Trimsaran Colliery, a few miles north-west of Llanelli, and around the end of the First World War he had the enterprise to provide a limited passenger service to and from Llanelli in his spare time. In due course the bus business became his main activity and the trunk Llanelli to Trimsaran to Carmarthen route was established in the early 1920s. Most of the competing operators were acquired over time and Eynon's developed a small route network built around two Llanelli to Carmarthen services with other routes spreading out to serve the intermediate Gwendraeth Valley villages and westward towards the coast at Kidwelly, famed for its prominent castle. Eynon's was taken over by Davies Bros, originally of Pencader, but by this time also with a Carmarthen base, in June 1988. Llanelli was a popular destination for passengers and this was the place to visit to see plenty of Eynon's red buses in service.

In Llanelli in May 1972 is (NNY 58), a Weymann-bodied Leyland PSUC1/1 that was new to Thomas Brothers of Port Talbot in 1954. The formation of the National Bus Company in 1969 caused major upheaval in the Swansea area. Neath & Cardiff, Thomas Bros and United Welsh were absorbed into the South Wales Transport Co on 1 January 1971, having been under SWT control since 1969.

Above: **Between 1955 and 1956 Plymouth Corporation took delivery of 48 Leyland PD2/12s with Metro-Cammell bodywork, numbered 31 to 78. Eynon's had at least three Plymouth Leyland PD2/12s in May 1973, (LCO 841, LCO 846 and LCO 847); the latter is seen in Llanelli, showing the destination Four Roads, a small village near Kidwelly, which, as the name suggests, is situated at a crossroads.**

Below: **Between 1953 and 1957 Western Welsh took delivery of 180 Weymann-bodied Leyland PSUC1/1s, numbered 1001 to 1180. The first of a batch of 50 delivered between 1956 and 1957 was (MUH 131), seen here in Carmarthen in May 1973 on an Eynon's service to Llanelli.**

Above: Many of Eynon's services were worked by double-deckers and, if their previous owner had also chosen a red livery, it was not uncommon for Eynon's to retain the colour scheme in which the buses were purchased, irrespective of the shade of red used, to minimise any repainting. Such examples include a batch of former Plymouth Corporation Leyland PD2/12s, some South Wales Transport AEC Regents and some Ribble Leyland Leopards. One of the South Wales AEC Regent Vs, originally

No 501 (RCY 343), with Weymann bodywork, is seen passing a well-kept garden in May 1973, descending from the village of Llansaint towards Kidwelly on the way to Llanelli.

Below: Another of Eynon's ex-South Wales Weymann-bodied AEC Regent Vs is (RCY 344), seen here in May 1973 between Trimsaran and Llanelli. The area between the decks may have been repainted cream, but the rest of the bus appears to still be in SWT red.

Gelligaer Urban District Council

Gelligaer was another of the small Glamorgan municipal fleets. The Council obtained powers to operate buses in 1921, but operations did not commence until 1928 when five buses were hired. The first buses purchased were Leylands and Albions, and in 1930 the first AECs were bought. No double-deck buses were operated until a few Daimler CWA6s with utility bodies arrived in 1944. Seven Bedford OWBs arrived during the war, but post-war deliveries returned to AEC and Leyland manufacture.

Above: **Seen in Caerphilly in April 1970 is Gelligaer No 23, (751 HNY). This Leyland PD2/40 was originally bodied by Longwell Green coachbuilders in 1960, and was given fleet number 14, but was subsequently rebodied by Caerphilly UDC in 1966/67.** *Geoff Gould*

Left: **Delivered to Gelligaer in 1963 were two Longwell Green-bodied AEC Reliances, Nos 10 (889 UTG) and 23 (890 UTG). This is No 10 at Bargoed in June 1973.** *Geoff Gould*

Above: Two Willowbrook-bodied AEC Reliances were delivered to Gelligaer in July 1964, Nos 13 (ANY 433B) and No 24 (ANY 432B). The former is seen at Cefn Hengoed in April 1970. The car parked behind is a Ford Zephyr 6 Mark III 213E. Unlike the Zephyr 4, the Zephyr 6 had a full-width grille including the headlight surrounds, but the overall body length and width were the same for both Zephyr III versions. Between 1962 and 1966 just over 105,000 of these cars were made. *Geoff Gould*

Below: In September 1972 Gelligaer received an order of three Bristol RESL6Gs with ECW bodies, Nos 42 to 44 (KTX 242L to KTX 244L). The last of the batch, No 44, is on a steep hill in Ystrad Mynach during June 1973. The car parked behind with the L plate is, I think, a Morris Oxford IV, which was made only as an estate; just over 58,000 were built between 1957 and 1960, this figure including the Series III estates, which were more 'woody'. Further up hill is a Ford Zephyr 4 Mark III, Model 211E. *Geoff Gould*

Opposite top: **During 1966 Gelligaer acquired two buses from Jones Omnibus Services, Aberbeeg: (TJU 686), a 1959 Duple-bodied AEC Reliance, and, seen here at Bargoed in June 1973, (UJU 774), a 1960 Willowbook-bodied AEC Reliance.** *Geoff Gould*

Below: **The first rear-engined double-deckers for Gelligaer were Nos 39 to 41 (BTX 539J to 541J), Bristol VRTSL6Gs bodied by Northern Counties. All three arrived in April 1971 and seen here in Newport, with the Rhymney Valley fleet name, in August 1974 is No 40 (BTX 540J). In the bay behind is Red & White No U262 (12 FAX), which was one of a batch of six Eastern Coachworks-bodied Bristol MW6Gs, new to Red & White in February 1963.** *Geoff Gould*

Opposite bottom: **Gelligaer took delivery of two more Willowbrook dual-doorway-bodied AEC Reliances, which arrived in November 1966. They were Nos 33 and 34 (LTG 733D and 734D) and the former is seen in Bargoed on 29 March 1975. At this time it is still in GUDC livery, but the Rhymney Valley fleet name is just visible above the wheel arch. The car to the left of the photograph is a Hillman Hunter.** *Geoff Gould*

Henley's

enley's was founded in Abertillery in 1948, and its first garage was located at the top end of Tillery Road and housed only one vehicle. It was not long before the move to Victor Road garage, which led to an increase in fleet size. By the 1970s the fleet size had grown and consisted of mini, service and luxury coaches, all in the tradition green and cream colours. Work covered included two service routes, factories, schools and excursion travel all around the county, and also the odd continental trip for good measure.

The old workshop that served the company so well is now long gone, replaced by a higher and more modern building where maintenance and service are carried out to the highest standards. The vehicle repair and fuel station located at the other end of Victor Road had been originally

Below: **During 1961 Western Welsh took delivery of 12 Willowbrook-bodied AEC Reliances, Nos 1276 to 1287. With Henley's by the mid-1970s, one of them, (WKG 287), is seen parked outside Henley's depot with the destination display showing Brynithel, a village perched high on the hillside above Llanhilleth, south of Abertillery.**

owned by Fairclough Funeral Directors and later by Roy & Gordon Hunt, who added a 24-hour breakdown recovery to the services. In the mid-1970s it was sold to Henley's and operated not just as a repair and fuel station, but also as the company's main reception and booking office for the coach hire. As the years have moved on, the minibus trend has been replaced by new luxury coaches covering thousands of miles per year. The service buses still run day in, day out, with the Cwmtillery to Brynithel services alone clocking up more than 70,000 miles per year.

Below: **Henley's still operate a small network of local routes within and around Abertillery, and Blaenau Gwent was a common sight as the destination on the company's buses. This photograph of (XAX 448), with 'Blaenau Gwent' on the linen, was taken as the bus returned from that estate to the town centre. Presumably to avoid confusion, the estate terminus is now referred to as Arael View. This bus is a former Jones of Aberbeeg Weymann-bodied AEC Reliance, which was new in 1960, and is still looking smart after 16 years in service.**

Jones (Aberbeeg)

T.W. W. Jones, an Aberbeeg collier, set up a bus company in 1921, and the first route operated was between the Cwm Hotel and Walpole Hotel, Llanhilleth. Because of competition, Jones moved to another route, Abertillery and Aberbeeg, and this was later extended to the Victoria Arms in Cwm. By 1925 Jones ran a route into the Cwmtillery Valley, and in 1927 part of this service was taken over by H.

Below: **Photographed in Ebbw Vale heading for Newport on a lovely summer's day in July 1972 is No 89 (VAX 362), a Leyland PSUC1/2, new to Jones in 1959.** *Geoff Gould*

J. Collier. In 1929 Mr Jones died and the business was taken over by Mrs E. Jones and her sons, trading as Jones Omnibus Services. On 12 March 1950 a tragedy hit the company when three of the directors were killed in a plane crash. The company then came under the directorship of Ron Jones and continued to expand. During April 1969 the company was sold to the National Bus Company together with 43 vehicles and around 50 services. The livery remained the same until 1973, but from that time on the blue and cream colours of Jones began to disappear.

Below: **Also seen in Ebbw Vale in July 1972 is No 99 (890 AAX), one of three Weymann-bodied** **Leyland PSUC1/3s delivered to Jones in 1961.** *Geoff Gould*

Below: **Near Cwm in July 1972, en route to Newport, is No 206, (KWO 206E) one of two Leyland PSUC1/12s with Willowbrook bodywork delivered in February 1967. Jones's fleet was all single-deckers, mostly Leyland Tiger Cubs and Leyland Leopards, the longer 33-foot and 36-foot Leopards being purchased to provide extra seats on the Newport service. Leyland Tiger Cubs were still being purchased up to 1969.** *Geoff Gould*

Above: **When Jones sold out to the National Bus Company in 1969, it was a surprise that control of the company, which favoured AEC and Leyland buses, passed to Red & White, when Jones had a close working relationship with Western Welsh. The Jones fleet livery remained, and seen here in July 1972 in Abertillery is No 114 (627 EWO), a Willowbrook-bodied AEC Reliance, delivered in 1962.**
Geoff Gould

David Jones (Abergwilli)

The business of David Jones started as a horse bus service in the 19th century and became one of the earliest operators of motor vehicles in Carmarthenshire. The bus operation expanded significantly in 1971 when Jones took over the Carmarthen town services of Western Welsh. Before that the company's main bus service had been between Carmarthen and Llandeilo, a route also served by Western Welsh on its longer route continuing via Llandovery to Brecon.

Opposite: **This is Carmarthen in May 1973, and working the Jones service to Llandeilo is KDB 690, which is heading from the railway station to the town centre stops to pick up for Llandeilo. This bus was new to North Western Road Car Company Limited in 1957 and is a Leyland PSUC1/1 bodied by Weymann. Just emerging from the right is a Morris FF/FH lorry. Launched in 1958 to replace the FE range, the FF came in 5-ton, 7-ton and 8-ton variants. The cab was new, with a contemporary wraparound windscreen taking the place of the FE's old-fashioned two-part screen with separate quarter-lights. The FH cab looked identical to the FF, but used a modified floorpan in order to accommodate a six-cylinder diesel engine. The FF/FH cab, and its Austin equivalent, the 45, were replaced in 1964 by the all-new FJ cab.**

Above: **Another Jones bus caught by the camera in Carmarthen in May 1973 is (MUH 150), a Weymann-bodied Leyland PSUC1/1, new to Western Welsh in 1956. The bus is in Carmarthen town centre working on the St David's Hospital local service, manoeuvring out of what is now part of a pedestrianised shopping precinct. David Jones & Son was taken over by Davies Bros of Pencader in April 1978.**

Llynfi Motors

In 1926 Llynfi started a route from Maesteg over the mountain to Port Talbot, and this route became the company's principal service throughout its existence. The route later benefited from the need to transport workers to and from the extensive steel works that were built at Port Talbot and also from the development of the sandy beach to the west of that town at Aberavon, which made this a more attractive summer destination. Each summer the Maesteg to Port Talbot route

Below: **Seen returning to Llynfi's depot in Maesteg in May 1973 is (JBO 104), a Weymann-bodied Leyland PSUC1/1 that was new to Western Welsh as its No 1104 in 1954. Parked in the background can be seen an example of Harrington Cavalier bodywork. The first Cavalier was body 2200, registered in February 1960 as (RNJ 900). As early as August 1959 firm contracts for ten coaches each were placed by Timpsons and Northern General, with smaller orders of four for East Yorkshire and three for South Wales Transport. Although the orders**

were in, Cavalier production did not get under way immediately. However, once started production soon gathered pace. The AEC Reliance was the most popular chassis and orders for the Cavalier remained strong right up until mid-1965, the last full year of factory production. Between 1971 and 1972 Llynfi purchased three AEC Reliance 2MU3RAs with Harrington Cavalier coach bodywork, which had been new in 1962 to Thomas Brothers of Port Talbot.

was extended to terminate at Aberavon Beach near the funfair. Llynfi Motors was acquired by Brewers, by then part of South Wales Transport, in July 1988. The extensions to Aberavon ceased many years ago and the Maesteg to Port Talbot route is now operated by First Cymru.

Above: On the same day in May 1973, just about to enter the depot, is (OTC 738), the first Leyland Tiger Cub produced, which had Saunders-Roe bodywork. The Tiger Cub was a lightweight chassis launched by Leyland in 1952 to counter criticism that the Royal Tiger was too heavy and thirsty. More than 4,500 Tiger Cubs were built up to 1969, by which time the model was being overtaken by the Leopard chassis. Saunders-Roe opened a factory at Fryars in Llanfaes, Anglesey, converting and maintaining Catalina flying boats. In the late 1940s and 1950s the Beaumaris factory began making bus bodies under the name of Saunders, for installing on Leyland Leopard and Leyland Tiger Cub chassis.

Above: **This is Aberavon Beach in the summer of 1964, and awaiting its return journey to Maesteg is Llynfi Motors (CHG 748), a Park Royal-bodied AEC Monocoach that was new to Ezra Laycock of Barnoldswick near Skipton in October 1954.**

Opposite above: **Leyland demonstrated its medium-weight Leopard chassis for the first time at the Scottish Motor Show in 1959. There were two versions on offer, the L1 and L2, both using the 0.600 horizontal engine, four-speed synchromesh gearbox, optional two-speed rear axle, and air brakes on all four wheels. Both models had an overall length of 30 foot and a width of 8 feet, but the L1 type had a straight rear extension designed for bus work,**

while the L2's dropped extension made it more suitable for coaches. Seen in Port Talbot during May 1973, bound for Maesteg, is Llynfi's (YNR 549), a Leyland L2, which began its working life as a Willowbrook demonstrator in October 1961. The bus has climbed from Port Talbot town centre to Pen-y-cae Road from where it will climb higher to the village of Bryn before dropping down into the Llynfi Valley and Maesteg. For some years Llynfi also had a small depot in Bryn.

Opposite below: **This is Station Road, Port Talbot, in September 1977, and working on a school contract is No 72 (YTG 304), a Massey-bodied Leyland PD3/4, which was delivered new to Llynfi in July 1958.**

Merthyr Tydfil Corporation

The Merthyr Tydfil Light Railways Order of 1899 authorised the construction of an electric tramway within the town, and the Merthyr Tydfil Electric Traction & Lighting Company Limited commenced operations on 6 April 1901, initially running between Cefn Bridge and Dowlais. Eventually some 3½ miles long, the tramway served Merthyr until 23 August 1939, when it was purchased by Merthyr Corporation and closed down. Merthyr Tydfil Council had obtained powers to operate buses in 1920, but these were not implemented until 1924. On 18 August 1924 the local

Below: **From 1958 to 1966 Merthyr Tydfil purchased 30 East Lancashire-bodied Leyland PD3s, and all were withdrawn by 1977. No 117 (CHB 117), however, one of eight Leyland PD3/5s new in October 1961, became a driver instruction vehicle, and is seen in Gadlys in early July 1977.** *Geoff Gould*

Above: **The last Leyland PD3s delivered to Merthyr, Nos 142 to 146 (CHB 407D to 411D), arrived during the period June to October** **1966. Seen on what looks like a very pleasant summer's day in July 1972 is the last of the batch, No 146.** *Geoff Gould*

authority commenced operating from Merthyr to Aberfan and Treharris, in competition with the many independents that were now running in the area. The livery was maroon and cream with a red waistband. On 22 August 1924 a second service, between Merthyr and Heolgerrig, was inaugurated, and on 3 September a service to Clwydyfagwyr began. On 7 May 1925 a service from Merthyr to Dowlais, via Pant and Caeracca started, followed shortly afterwards on 25 August by one from Merthyr to Twynyrodyn. On 8 September 1930 a through service to Cardiff commenced, jointly with Cardiff

Corporation, although two independents (Rhondda Tramways and Imperial Motor Services) were also licensed to operate on the route. Wartime deliveries included ten Daimler CWA6s, which was an unusually large number for such a small fleet.

Following the end of the war there was considerable redevelopment in the centre of the town, new estates were constructed in out-of-town areas and the fleet was expanded accordingly as new services were introduced. Bristol vehicles were favoured until they became unavailable, although a batch of six (Nos 47-52) Foden PVD6s was purchased in 1948. In the early 1950s,

Above: The Leyland Leopard was first introduced in 1959 and had the Leyland 0.600 engine fitted; the first Leopards were designated L1, for use as a bus, and L2, as a coach. However, it should be noted that L1s were bodied as coaches and L2s as buses. When 36-foot buses were legalised for road use in 1961, the PSU3 series was introduced, with the important option of a semi-automatic transmission. The 0.680 engine was introduced to semi-automatic-transmission buses from 1966, although the 0.600 was still available until 1973. Seen here when new in July 1972 is No 180 (HHB 180K), one of five East Lancashire-bodied Leyland PSU3B/2Rs delivered during mid-1972. The PSU3B code indicates that this bus has a Maudslay rear axle in place of an Eaton, and revised brake linings. One of this batch of buses, No 183, was owned by Parfitts from 1989, and has now passed into preservation. *Geoff Gould*

following the appointment of a new manager, the livery was changed to dark red with cream relief.

The purchase of a Leyland PD2/12 demonstrator (No 70) in 1954 (the first 8-foot-wide bus in the fleet) led to a standardisation on Leyland vehicles that continued for many years. In 1967 the livery was again revised to predominantly cream with red relief and was applied to most of the single-deckers, although it was considered unsuitable for double-deckers, which remained in the red with cream relief livery. A move to low-floor buses was made in 1973, resulting in the purchase of two Metro-Scanias, which, because of their high fuel consumption, lasted just five years in the fleet, and four Bristol RESL6Gs, a marque that had recently been reintroduced to the marketplace after previously being restricted to the nationalised sector.

Below: **Metro-Scania was a name coined by MCW to reflect the combination of Scania running units with bodywork by MCW. The Scania BR111/MCW Metro-Scania was built in Sweden and Birmingham from 1969 until 1973, and was a semi-integral vehicle based on the Scania BR110/1 and CR110 chassis. Among the main customers for this bus were Newport and Leicester Corporations. Two Metro-Scanias, Nos 186 and 187 (KHB 186L and 187L) were delivered to Merthyr in April 1973, and seen here on 1 August 1977 in the orange livery introduced in 1974 is No 186. Both buses were withdrawn in 1978.** *Geoff Gould*

Newport Corporation

Newport Corporation purchased the Newport Tramways Company in 1894, and by 1898 22 cars were in operation being worked by 118 horses. In 1903 electric tramcars appeared, and ten years later 29 tramcars were operating on six routes. Gradual abandonment of the tramcars started in 1928, and the last ran in 1937. The first buses were Karriers, introduced in 1924, followed by Leyland and Guy buses. During the war a number of Guys and Daimlers to utility specifications were added to the fleet, then after the war most new buses ordered were Leylands.

Below: **During 1973 London Transport purchased six Metro-Scanias, MS1 to MS6 (PGC 201L to 206L). MS1 arrived at Aldenham in April 1973 and was then transferred to Chiswick for testing. The bus entered service on route S2 from Dalston in August 1973, but by June 1976 it was stored, staying so for nearly two years before being withdrawn in May 1978. Newport Corporation purchased MS1 in November 1978, but it was never used and was dismantled for spares by February 1980. No MS2 was withdrawn in May 1978 and was sold in November 1980 to Allco in Ruislip. It was then purchased by Black Prince of Morley for spares and was later acquired for preservation. The remaining Metro-Scanias, MS3 to MS6, were all purchased by Newport in November 1978, and numbered 103 to 106. No 104 (PGC 204L) entered service in January 1979, and is seen here at Ringland in mid-1979. This bus was bought for preservation in 1991. No 106 was not so fortunate, as it was burned out and scrapped in 1983.** *Geoff Gould*

Above: **Seen at the Castle roundabout in August 1974 is the first of a batch of nine Alexander J-Type-bodied Leyland PDR1/1s, No 10 (TDW 310J), new to Newport Corporation during April and May 1971. Travelling behind is one of the 1970 Alexander A-Type-bodied Leyland PDR1/1s that were delivered in January 1970, and a Metro-Scania.** *Geoff Gould*

Below: **As far as I am aware, one of the Metro-Scania demonstrators, VWD 451H or VWD 452H, was loaned to Newport Transport for demonstration purposes. The Corporation subsequently decided to purchase a large batch of 44 Scania BR111MHs with MCW B40D bodywork between 1971 and 1972. Seen in Dock Street in August 1972 is one of these, No 57 (YDW 757K).** *Geoff Gould*

Above: **Newport Corporation Nos 72 to 76 were originally to be registered (EDW 72D) to EDW 76D, but because they were delivered in July 1967 they were re-registered HDW 772E to (HDW 776E). They were Alexander-bodied Leyland PDR1/1s, and seen here in Dock Street in August 1972 is No 72.** *Geoff Gould*

Right: **Looking, I think, very smart is No 107 (JDW 307F), one of a batch of eight Bristol RESL6s with Eastern Coachwork bodies and Leyland engines that were new to Newport in September 1967. This photograph was taken at the Castle roundabout during August 1974. Newport Castle is a 14th-century stone rectangular courtyard fortress, founded by Hugh d'Audele. In the 15th century Humphrey Stafford strengthened the castle, but sadly only the east front now survives. The high curtain wall, flanked by a central tower with a watergate and two octagonal angle towers with spur buttresses, stands on the west bank of the River Usk.** *Geoff Gould*

Right: **The main housing estate at Maesglas was built in the 1930s, when the winters were of such severity that the workmen gave it the name 'Moscow'. Carrying a very healthy number of passengers to Maesglas in August 1974 is No 96 (PDW 96H), an Alexander-bodied Leyland PDR1A/1. The first Alexander A-type body, as on No 96, was built in September 1963 and was Graham of Paisley's No 61 (HXS 85).** *Geoff Gould*

Peakes

Peakes ceased operating bus services in March 1987 and National Welsh took over its commercial Pontypool routes. Later there was a period of competition between National Welsh and a new operator, Phil Anslow. Stagecoach is now the principal operator in the town.

Below: **The operation of Pontypool local services was hampered by the lack of opportunities for full-size buses to turn in the town centre, and the Clarence Bus Park, well to the south of the busiest part of the town centre, was used as a bus terminus. Working for Peakes in Pontypool in midsummer 1973 is MUH 135, an ex-Western Welsh Weymann-bodied Leyland PSUC1/1 dating from 1956. Clarence Bus Park is no more, the site and adjoining area having been redeveloped as part of a bypass scheme and a Tesco supermarket.**

Above: **Between 1952 and 1957 both Southern and Western National took delivery of large numbers of Bristol LSs with five-cylinder Gardner engines. Representative of this type of bus is (LTA 977), originally new to Western National as its No W1680 in 1952, and seen here working for Peakes and approaching Clarence Bus Park in Pontypool in August 1974.**

Above: **Also working the Pontypool to Abersychan service of Peakes on the same day as the previous picture is (ARN 590C). Ribble Motor Services took delivery of 60 Leyland PSU3/1Rs in 1965 with bodywork by either Marshall or Weymann. This particular bus was new to Ribble as its No 590 in June 1965, and has bodywork by Weymann.**

Pontypridd Urban District Council

Authority to construct a tramway in Pontypridd was given under the Pontypridd & Rhondda Valley Tramways Order of 1882. The Pontypridd & Rhondda Valley Tramways Company was eventually purchased on 31 October 1904 and the tramway officially opened on 5

Below: **The Guy Arab LUF was a lightweight underfloor-engined bus or coach chassis that could accommodate up to 45 passengers. Pontypridd Urban District Council purchased a total of four, with Roe rear-entrance bodywork. Three, Nos 77 to 79 (VNY 655 to 657) arrived in 1957, and seen on Broadway in March 1973, with well steamed-up windows, is No 77.** *Geoff Gould*

March 1905, running from the town centre to Treforest railway station, with a branch line connecting to Cilfynydd, which was worked as a single route via Pontypridd. In 1908 the tramway was connected to the Rhondda system at the Trehafod boundary, where passengers were required to change cars until July 1919, when through running commenced, although this was abandoned in December 1927.

In 1929 Pontypridd UDC obtained powers to operate motorbuses and trolleybuses and, on 18 September 1930, the Treforest to Cilfynydd section was converted to trolleybus operation. Seven single-deck 32-seat English Electric

trolleybuses formed the initial fleet. The following year, 30 August 1931, the remaining line to Trehafod was closed and motorbuses took over, the through service to Porth being operated jointly with Rhondda. The first motorbus service had commenced in June the previous year when a service between Pontypridd and Rhydyfelin had been inaugurated using four Bristol B-Type single-deckers. The Bristol chassis subsequently became a regular choice for Pontypridd UDC.

The new trolleybus service proved extremely popular, so much so that at busy periods it was necessary to supplement the trolleybuses with tramcars, so the exact date of the last tram is uncertain. Additional trolleybuses were soon purchased and in early 1931 a pair of demonstrators arrived. The first was a Guy BTX with Guy H59R bodywork, followed shortly afterwards by a Bristol E with Beadle H60R bodywork, one of only two ever built. Both demonstrators were purchased in 1932. The trolleybus service was now established and continued unchanged until the advent of the Second World War, when wartime demands saw several trolleybuses arrive on loan.

Further motorbus services were established throughout the 1930s, principally to Caerphilly (jointly with Caerphilly UDC), to Ynysybwl (jointly with Rhondda and Red & White), and to the Treforest Trading Estate, which was established to entice alternative industries to the area in view of the high unemployment in the coal-mining industry. In 1945 Pontypridd ordered eight Karrier trolleybuses to replace the ageing fleet; delivery began in March 1945 and was completed towards the end of 1946. In 1955, however, with

the trolleybuses regularly being replaced by motorbuses when out of service, delays in the delivery of new motorbuses meant that the final abandonment of the trolleybus system did not take place until 31 January 1957. All the trolleybuses were sold for service elsewhere.

Above: **In the late afternoon sunshine of October 1973 we see No 81 (502 ATX), one of three smart Roe-bodied Guy Arab IVs new to Pontypridd in 1958.** *Geoff Gould*

Until 1950 the Council operated a largely Bristol fleet, but deliveries from 1950 until 1961 were Guys. New vehicles arriving in the fleet from 1961 included the AEC Reliance, which was to become the standard single-deck vehicle, and the AEC Regent V, which was purchased as the standard double-decker.

Right: **Seen in Broadway in March 1973 is No 95 (JNY 366D), the first of two Willowbrook-bodied AEC Reliances, which arrived in March 1966. From 1960 the Mini range included an estate car version, seen on the left, which was built on a longer wheelbase that it shared with the Mini Van and Pick-up. The estate came as either the Austin Seven Countryman or the Morris Mini Minor Traveller, both versions being identical apart from the badges. The longer wheelbase enabled the Mini estate versions to offer a reasonable load-carrying area, which benefited from having a fold-flat rear bench seat. Early Countryman/Travellers came with a wood exterior frame at the rear, similar to the Morris Minor Traveller, although the wood was not structural in any way.** *Geoff Gould*

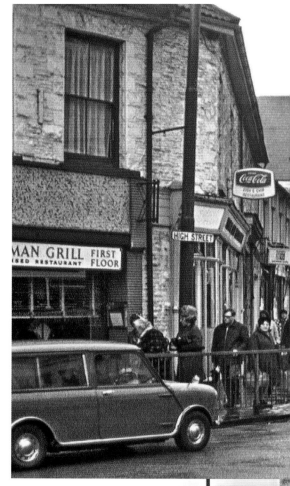

Below: **Under local government reorganisation in April 1974, Pontypridd UDC became Taff-Ely District Council. The Transport Department was little changed, but assumed the name of the new District Council. Nos 89 (seen here) and 90 (997 and 998 TTX) were AEC Reliances delivered in 1963, but this time bodied by Longwell Green. In the background is Leyland National No 22 (MBO 22P), one of 18 Nationals purchased between 1973 and 1980.** *Geoff Gould*

Opposite top: **In February 1962 two AEC Reliances with Roe bodywork, Nos 85 and 86 (951 and 952 MTX) entered service with Pontypridd, and seen here in March 1973 is No 85. A few yards behind it is a Humber Sceptre, a model introduced by Rootes in 1967 using a twin-carb 1725cc engine and other mechanical parts from the more basic Hillman Hunter. Externally the Sceptre featured quad headlamps, a traditional chrome grille and other 'luxuries' such as twin reversing lights. Inside it featured a beautiful walnut fascia and comfortable seats trimmed in hard-wearing vinyl material. The Humber Sceptre proved to be a popular model with retiring executives and continued in production until 1976 when it, and the Humber marque, were discontinued. Between 1967 and 1976 a total of 43,951 were produced.** *Geoff Gould*

Opposite bottom: **During 1967 Pontypridd took delivery of seven Metro-Cammell-bodied AEC Regent Vs, Nos 1 to 6 (NNY 758E to 763E) and No 99 (NNY 757E). In Gelliwastad Road in March 1973 is No 6, and in the background is one of the 1957 Roe-bodied Guy Arab LUFs. The cars are either Morris Oxfords or Austin Cambridges.** *Geoff Gould*

Below: **Willowbrook had the distinction of bodying the last Regent Vs built for the home market; two were delivered to Douglas Corporation in December 1968 and two to Pontypridd Urban District Council in March 1969. Seen at Rhydyfelin in October 1975 is the last AEC Regent V, No 8 (UTG 313G).** *Geoff Gould*

Porthcawl Omnibus

Early transport in Porthcawl consisted mainly of runabouts with either 7 or 14 seats, and there were a number of operators providing these services in the 1920s and 1930s. After the Second World War a number of these operators grouped together to form the Porthcawl Motor Omnibus Co Ltd and, with the purchase of A. Shute, a local monopoly was created. Subsequently the company was acquired by Kenfig Motors. In 1977 it again changed hands, coming under the control of John Williams, a former Porthcawl driver who

Below: **The Esplanade in the centre of Porthcawl looks out over a rocky beach, but there are extensive stretches of sandy beaches both to the east and the west of the town at Trecco Bay and Rest Bay respectively. Trecco Bay has a large caravan and holiday camp, while Rest Bay, as the name might imply, is more rural and less developed, and has become very popular with surfers in recent years. Porthcawl Omnibus operated bus services between the town and both beaches. Rest Bay journeys picked up at a stop on The Esplanade, which is where these passengers are boarding Leyland Olympic (MTG 469) during the summer of 1964. In the background is the Pavilion Theatre, still a venue for popular stage shows today.**

had left the company in 1965 to operate several former Porthcawl services that had previously been Western Welsh services in the area. From 1986 the livery was changed from white and maroon to maroon and beige. A varied second-hand fleet has always been operated, and all vehicles were operated from the Old Station Lane Depot on four routes from Porthcawl, together with several local routes and a summer service to the local holiday camp. Porthcawl Omnibus only operated within that town until about 1985 or 1986 when, with deregulation looming, it introduced a route to Bridgend competing with National Welsh. Other out-of-town routes, including a regular limited stop service to Cardiff, only came later.

Above: **This excellent view was taken in 1964 and shows (ACM 319), a Massey-bodied Leyland PD1, new to Birkenhead Corporation in 1948, picking up passengers at the town centre terminus for Trecco Bay at the side of the Esplanade Hotel. A few years ago the hotel was rebuilt as a block of upmarket flats of a modern angular design, which many feel is out of keeping with the more genteel architecture of this part of Porthcawl. But the residents do enjoy, as did holidaymakers of old, marvellous views across the Bristol Channel to the Quantock and Exmoor hills. The Leyland PD1 was withdrawn by Birkenhead Corporation in 1961. Leyland Olympic (MTG 469) is turning from The Esplanade into Mary Street, having returned from Rest Bay.**

Above: **Western Welsh was a keen purchaser of Leyland Olympics, and during 1956 a total of 40 Weymann-bodied Leyland HRC40s were delivered. On what looks like a very pleasant day in July 1972 one of this batch, (LKG 206), now working for Porthcawl Omnibus, is seen crossing Locks Common on the West Park town route, which served the modern residential estates set well back from Rest Bay, some of which are just visible in the background. The Leyland Olympic single-decker was introduced in 1949 in conjunction with MCW as an integral underfloor-engined alternative to the Tiger. Designated the HR40 Olympic ('40' denoting the seating capacity), it used a horizontal version of the 0.600 engine. In 1951, when length regulations were relaxed to allow 30-foot single-deckers on two axles, it became the HR44, a 44-seater.**

Red & White Services

During the years 1921-22 John Watts of Lydney in Gloucestershire started two bus companies, Gloucestershire Transport, which ran local bus services around Lydney, and The Valleys Motor Bus Services, which ran buses around Tredegar in South Wales. Both companies expanded rapidly by acquiring nearby operators. In 1926 the Lydney business adopted the name Gloster (Red & White) Services, and by 1928 the companies were operating buses between Gloucester, Hereford and South Wales. On 1 January 1930 John Watts formed Red & White Services Ltd to bring together the various bus companies he had formed or

Above: **Red & White had, I think, a wonderful numbering system, consisting of a class identifier (usually one or two letters), then a dot, followed by the number of the bus in the batch and ending with the two numbers identifying the year when it was new. Thus, this Eastern Coachworks-bodied Bristol MW6G, UC1758 (SWO 988), was an underfloor-engined coach, the seventeenth bus in the batch, and was new in 1958. Seen in Bridgwater in August 1972, U1758 was part of a batch of 17 delivered between May and September 1958, arriving in May 1958. The Plaxton-bodied AEC Reliance on the right, (TDK 684J), was new to Yelloway of Rochdale in 1971.** *Geoff Gould*

acquired.

In 1929 Red & White entered the long-distance coach market, initially from Gloucester and between London and South Wales. In the early 1930s coach operators were acquired further afield, with services between London, Liverpool and Glasgow, and between Cardiff and Blackpool, and in 1934 Red & White was one of the founder members of the Associated Motorways consortium. The company expanded rapidly during the 1930s, by now from new headquarters in Chepstow. It acquired several bus companies in the Swansea area and elsewhere in South Wales.

In 1933 Red & White acquired the business of Red Bus Services of Stroud, and by 1937 Red & White and its subsidiaries were operating a fleet of more than 400 buses and coaches. In that year Red & White United Transport Ltd was formed as a public company to hold the group's various interests. The group's operations in the Swansea area were brought together in 1939 in a new company, United Welsh Services Ltd. Later in 1939 the group

Below: **During 1954 Bristol introduced a new small-capacity bus for rural routes, the SC4LK, with Gardner's smallest engine. These vehicles were of a lightweight design – even the main chassis members were constructed in aluminium. They were designed for a service life of around ten years, although many well outlasted that time. With their frugal four-cylinder Gardner oil engines, they were best suited to flat areas of service. Only four Bristol SC4LKs were delivered new to Red & White, which also purchased three second-hand from United Counties in 1963 (ONV 425 to 427). The four were delivered in November 1957 and were numbered SC157 to SC457 (SAX 473 to SAX 476). Representing this class in the Red & White fleet is (SAX 473), seen in Abergavenny in 1967. Standing next in line is a Weymann-bodied Albion Nimbus of Western Welsh, and furthest away is one of a pair of MCW-bodied Leyland Olympic HR 40s that were new to Red & White in 1950. The last Bristol SC4LK was delivered to Lincolnshire in August 1961, and a new small underfloor-engined chassis was introduced, with 30 seats (SUS) or 36 seats (SUL).** *Geoff Gould*

Above: The Bristol FL was a very rare bus indeed, only 42 being produced between October 1960 and January 1963. As delivered, 30 had Gardner engines and 12 Bristol engines. The first company to receive them was Red & White, which took delivery of 20 with Gardner engines in October 1960, numbered L160 to L2060 (VAX 508, VAX 509 and 3 AAX to 20 AAX). Just about to leave Abergavenny in the summer of 1967 is (VAX 509). *Geoff Gould*

Below: In all, Red & White purchased 20 Bristol FSs, which were delivered with a mixture of Gardner and Bristol engines. The last four to arrive were between July and August 1964, and they were numbered L863 to L1163 (AAX 22B to AAX 25B). Looking very smart in Newport in August 1974 is the last of the 1964 batch, (AAX 25B), which was delivered with a Bristol engine. *Geoff Gould*

bought Cheltenham District Traction Company. Expansion continued even during the Second World War: in early 1944 the group bought Newbury & District, which ran buses in west Berkshire, and in 1945 it acquired Venture Ltd, the main bus operator in Basingstoke, Hampshire. Also in 1945 it bought South Midland Motor Services of Oxford, which before the war had run express coach services between London, Oxford and Worcester.

In common with many other operators during the period 1938 to 1950, Red & White felt that nationalisation was inevitable, and in 1950 offered the entire group to the British Transport Commission. The BTC subsequently transferred most of the English bus operations of Red & White to other recently nationalised companies. Venture Ltd was transferred to Wilts &

Dorset, and Newbury & District and the management of South Midland were transferred to Thames Valley Traction. The operations in the Stroud area and Cheltenham District Traction Company were transferred to Bristol Tramways. In return, the Forest of Dean services of Bristol Tramways were transferred to Red & White. This left Red & White with its services in Monmouthshire, the Forest of Dean and the Glamorgan valleys. United Welsh was managed separately within the BTC.

In 1962 Red & White was transferred to the state-owned Transport Holding Company, and in 1969 to the National Bus Company. In 1978 the NBC merged the operations of Red & White into the neighbouring NBC operator Western Welsh, which became National Welsh.

Below: **Between March and April 1967 Red & White purchased 21 Bristol RESL6s with Leyland engines – RS 167 to RS 2167 (LAX 101E** **to 121E). Loading passengers at Merthyr Tydfil bus station for a service to Cardiff in July 1972 is RS 2067 (LAX 120E).** *Geoff Gould*

Rees & Williams

Rees & Williams Ltd of Tycroes, a village just south of Ammanford, dated from 1926 when an existing bus-operating partnership between the two families was formally constituted into a limited company. But within a few years there was disagreement between the owners and some members of the Williams family set up a competing bus company, West Wales Motors, in the same village, a situation that continued for about 60 years. The licensing of bus services introduced by the 1930 Road Traffic Act brought about some rationalisation of the competing services, and in this area the outcome was several jointly operated services. Rees & Williams shared two main services with other firms and both routes were generally operated by double-deckers at hourly intervals except on Sundays. The Llandeilo to Ammanford and Swansea service required three buses, and Rees & Williams, South Wales Transport and West Wales provided one each. The Llanelli to Ammanford and Llanelli route also needed three vehicles, but here the arrangement was two buses from Rees & Williams and one from South Wales Transport. Both routes had the operational advantage of passing Rees & Williams's premises in Tycroes.

Below: **Sunday services on both routes were irregular, and the Llanelli route (No 16) was by 1964 being operated by a sole Rees & Williams bus, although as shown by this photo of (ETH 104) (a Guy Arab II rebodied by Massey during 1958) it was still a double-decker. The Sunday timetable at this time on the Swansea route (No 36) was worked by one Rees & Williams and one West Wales bus, timings being clearly aimed at taking passengers into Swansea rather than**

offering residents of that town an opportunity to travel to the countryside; departures from Swansea were at 15.15 (R&W), 15.35 (WW), 18.35 (R&W) and 20.05 (WW). The closeness of the two afternoon departures was governed by visiting times at local hospitals, the West Wales working being extended to and from Morriston Hospital a few miles north of the town centre, the bus arriving there at 13.55 and leaving at 15.15, departing from St Mary's Church at 15.35. It is noteworthy that South Wales Transport did not participate in the Sunday operation on either route.

Below: In 1950 Guy presented the Arab IV, and Lancashire United was the first operator to purchase this model, with Weymanm 57-seat bodies; other operators included Chester, Southdown, Birmingham (which bought more than 300 examples), Cardiff and Sunderland (with Crossley bodies), Exeter (with Massey 57- and 58-seat bodywork), and East Kent. At first designed to meet the needs of Birmingham City Transport, the Arab IV came with a 27-foot-long body and a 16ft 4in wheelbase, available in 7ft 6in of 8-foot widths. During 1956 a 30-foot-long chassis with an 18ft 6 in wheelbase was introduced when the law allowed it. Arab IVs received power from a variety of engines: the Gardner 5LW and 6LW and Meadows 10.35-litre 6DC630. Brakes were either of the vacuum-aided triple-servo variety or air brakes, as, for example, with the 30-foot-long chassis. There was some overlap in production of the Marks III and IV until 1953, in which year an exposed radiator was available for Mark IV buses for those customers who favoured this version. Production of the Arab IV was discontinued in 1960, although some buses were built in 1962, but by then the Wulfrunian and Arab Mark V were challenging the popularity of their predecessor. In the town of Pontarddulais in May 1973 is Rees & Williams (UTH 78), a Massey low-height-bodied Guy Arab IV that the company purchased new in January 1960.

Above: **Sentinel was a premier maker of steam trucks, and went on to look at diesel vehicles in a different way from most others, coming up with the underfloor-engined diesel truck and the very first underfloor-engined bus. After the war Sentinel was purchased by Metal Industries Group, which, as part of its business, supplied panelling to the Kent bodybuilder Beadle, and this partnership entered into bus-building. Sentinel's biggest single customer was Ribble, which purchased 20 between 1949 and 1951. When the dimensions regulations were relaxed to allow 30-foot vehicles, Sentinel introduced its STC6 integral bus. It used a six-cylinder 9.12-litre 135bhp indirect injection engine, with a four-speed constant-mesh gearbox. The well-known firm of Ribble was the most significant customer for the Sentinel STC6, acquiring 14 44-seat models built in 1951, despite the fact that the Olympic was now available from its usual supplier, Leyland. Acquired by Rolls-Royce in 1955, Sentinel stopped production of coaches and buses in 1956, having only produced around 130 buses in total for the domestic market. Standing alongside St Mary's Church in Swansea, having arrived at 13.53 on a Sunday afternoon and ready to form the 15.15 departure, is Rees & Williams Sentinel (KBX 630).**

Above: **Rees & Williams ordered another Guy Arab IV with Massey bodywork, (YTH 315), and this arrived in January 1962. Seen here in May 1972, it was unusual in South Wales as it had a Johannesburg-style front; the only other buses in South Wales to have this design of radiator were two Roe-bodied Guys purchased by Pontypridd Urban District Council. This bus was subsequently operated by Green Bus Service (Warstone) of Staffordshire.**

Below: **In 1959 Northern General Transport received a batch of 20 Willowbrook-bodied Leyland PSUC1/1s. A few miles north-west of Swansea is the small town of Pontarddulais, and ex-Northern General No 1888 (JCN 888), now in the ownership of Rees & Williams, is seen there en route to Llanelli.**

Richards Brothers

The company commenced operating as W. G. Richards & Sons of Brodawel, Moylgrove. W. G. Richards was a general haulage contractor with a steam engine, and was offered a contract with Higgs & Hill when RNAD Trecwn was being built. He carried workmen in 14-seat vans to the construction site, in a valley 3 miles

Above: **During 1955 and 1956 Southdown received a batch of 12 Park Royal-bodied Leyland PD2/12s, its Nos 765 to 776 (OCD 765 to 776). No 771 (OCD 771) was acquired by Richards in August 1968 and is seen here leaving Aberporth RAF Station on a works service in May 1973. By November of that year it was reported as being with a dealer, and was subsequently sold for scrap.**

south of Fishguard. The company's first true bus was a Bedford OWB utility bus with wooden seats bought in May 1943. Mr Richards's sons Reggie and Idris then joined the business, and Richards Bros was formed. After the depot was completed, contracts were obtained to convey workmen from the Moylgrove, St Dogmaels and Cardigan areas to the depot. These vehicles were then used to convey prisoners of war to outlying farms from a camp in Letterston. School contracts were then obtained, and more buses purchased. The first of several company acquisitions occurred in 1958 with Owen Williams of Cardigan; that company's operation to the north of the town provided Richards Bros with its first local services.

In 1971 Western Welsh withdrew from the area and Richards Bros took over the Fishguard to St David's service. In 1972 the business of Lewis Williams (Blue Glider) of St Dogmaels was acquired, and in 1976 a very old rival company, Pioneer Motors of Newport (a company for which one of the partners, Reggie, had worked for many years) was purchased. In 1978 a new workshop and office was built in Newport to accommodate the extra servicing facilities required. In 1982 the business of Marchwood Motorways, Southampton, which had a depot in Haverfordwest, was purchased, and more local services were acquired. In 1984 the Moylgrove depot was closed and a new head office set up in Pentood Industrial Estate, Cardigan, with a paint shop and garage. In 1998 the coaching side of T. M. Daniel of Cardigan was purchased.

Today, Richard Brothers bus services operate between Haverfordwest, Milford Haven, St David's, Cardigan, Aberystwyth and Carmarthen, with coaches travelling all over Europe, and the company employs 70 staff with 65 vehicles.

Rhondda Transport Co

The Rhondda Tramways Company Limited was incorporated on 14 April 1906, and by April 1912 the total mileage of the tramway was 28¾. In late 1914 trolleybuses were introduced, but due to serious road difficulties the service was terminated in March 1915 and the Brush trolleybuses purchased for the service were sold to Tees-side. On 5 August 1920 nine second-hand buses were purchased to provide a bus service to Clydach Vale. The bus routes were expanded throughout the decade, and by 1928 49 single-deck buses were in service. As a result of this expansion, the last trams ran on 1 February 1934 and the company changed its name to the Rhondda Transport Company Limited on 13 August, with a fleet of 106 buses. In pre-war years they were a mixture of Bristol, Dennis, Leyland and AEC vehicles, but the war years saw the introduction of Daimler and Guy utilities to the fleet. During the 1960s the fleet consisted mainly of Leyland Tiger Cubs, while the double-decker fleet were AECs.

Below: **During 1964 Rhondda took delivery of ten Northern Counties-bodied AEC Regent Vs, Nos 469 to 478 (469 to 478 UNY). Seen in Porthcawl in the summer of 1967 is one of this batch, No 471. Between 1956 and 1966 Rhondda purchased 98 AEC Regent V double-deckers.** *Geoff Gould*

Below: **This 'scenic' shot was taken in the Rhondda Fach valley in 1969. Most of the houses and the main road in the upper Rhondda Fach cling to the western side of the valley, with the river and the former railway line in the bottom, although there are a few isolated communities on the eastern side. Blaenllechau is one such community, and this view was taken there, showing a bus negotiating the hairpin bend on the ascent to the village. The bus is from** one of the batches of Leyland Tiger Cubs with Marshall bodywork, either (HTG 300 to 303D), delivered new to Rhondda in 1966, or RTG 304F to 315F, new in 1968. I think it is surprising that Rhondda concentrated on AECs for its double-deckers, but apparently not for single-deckers. Perhaps Reliances boiled too easily in such hilly terrain? *Geoff Gould*

Above: **This is Morgan Street in Pontypridd in the summer of 1971, and Rhondda No 473 (473 UNY), a 1964 Northern Counties AEC Regent V, is supposedly on a working of the Rhondda route 520 from Pontypridd to Porth, then to Blaencwm. The Rhondda Transport Company was absorbed into Western Welsh in that year, but as yet No 473 has not received its new fleet number, livery or lettering. Parked at the side of the road is a Pontypridd UDC Roe-bodied Guy Arab in the light blue livery of that operator, which was introduced in 1971.** *transporttreasury.co.uk*

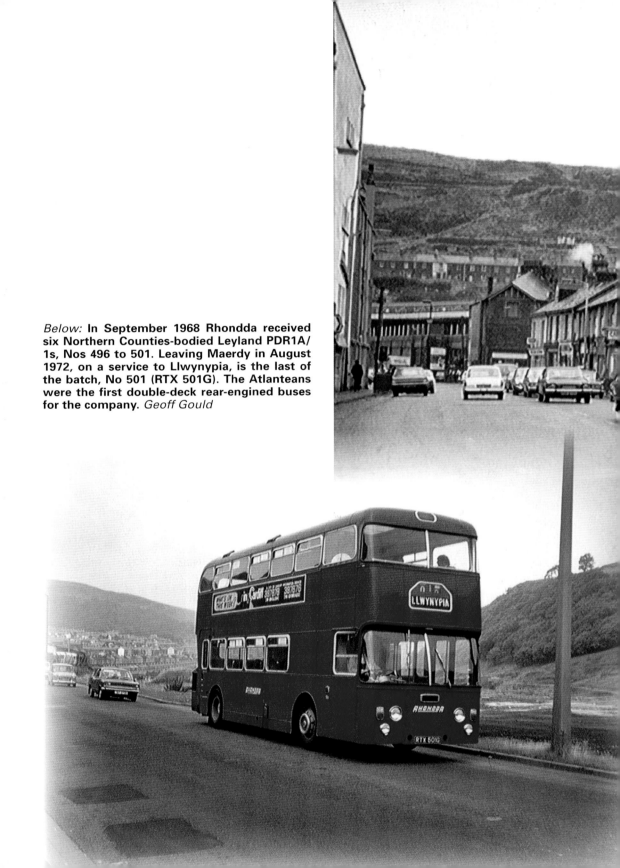

Below: **In September 1968 Rhondda received six Northern Counties-bodied Leyland PDR1A/ 1s, Nos 496 to 501. Leaving Maerdy in August 1972, on a service to Llwynypia, is the last of the batch, No 501 (RTX 501G). The Atlanteans were the first double-deck rear-engined buses for the company.** *Geoff Gould*

Above: **The halcyon days of the Rhondda Transport Company were coming to an end, and there was a gradual increase in the ownership of motor cars and a decrease in the workforce in Rhondda's factories, such as Polikoff and EMI. The company was bought out by the management, but in January 1971 was taken over by the Western Welsh Bus Company. This became National Welsh on 27 April 1978, but** following the collapse of the company Rhondda Buses was formed in 1992. This company survived for five years before becoming part of the Stagecoach group in 1997. In January 1971 Western Welsh took delivery of buses ordered by Rhondda; they were Nos 512 to 520, Alexander J-Type-bodied Leyland PDR1A/1s. Still in Rhondda livery in Pontypridd in March 1973 is No 518 (BTG 518J). *Geoff Gould*

Silcox Motor Coach Co

William Luther Silcox, a saddler, established the company in 1882. By 1939, when new office and garage premises were opened at Waterloo on the edge of Pembroke Dock, the firm was trading as W. L. Silcox & Sons. Since 1932 Silcox had operated bus services around Pembrokeshire, and local bus and coach services expanded during the 1930s. The Second World War saw much transport of workers and servicemen, and the company had its first double-deckers allocated under the Ministry of Supply rationing scheme, some second-hand, and the inevitable Guy Arab 1s.

After the war Army and Navy establishments continued to generate a demand for local recreational journeys together with long-distance services for personnel going on leave. In the 1950s and 1960s the oil industry boom led to many contracts to carry construction workers and serve oil refineries, replacing the armed forces traffic that was running down with

Below: **In Tenby in May 1973 is (OTT 52), an Eastern Coachworks-bodied Bristol LS5G new to Southern National as its No S1678 during 1954 and acquired by Silcox from Cream Line of Tonmawr, near Neath. Just behind the bus is a Triumph Spitfire. This was a small two-seat sports car introduced in 1962, based on a design produced for Standard-Triumph in 1957 by Italian designer Giovanni Michelotti. The car was largely based on the Triumph Herald saloon, and throughout its life was built at the Standard-Triumph works at Canley in Coventry. I think this Spitfire is a Mark III, introduced in 1967, which had a 1296cc engine instead of a 1147cc unit. The Mark III was the fastest Spitfire yet, achieving 60mph in 12.5 seconds, and the Mark III actually continued production into 1970, well after the Mark IV was introduced. Between 1967 and 1970 a total of 65,320 of this mark were produced.**

the closure of bases and the ending of National Service. In March 1963 the partnership was converted into a Private Limited Liability Company, the Silcox Motor Coach Company Limited.

The 1970s saw the withdrawal of major operators from West Wales, and Silcox filled the gap, while centralisation of education demanded a substantial fleet of school buses. Silcox had a large number of Bristols for an independent fleet, which gave the company a unique character, enhanced by the fact that ten of them were bodied 'in-house'. Silcox also bought many second-hand Bristols. Although only ten bodies were built by Silcox from scratch, major rebuilding and refurbishment in its own workshops has always been a feature.

Only in recent years has the carrying

Above: **This excellent study of (MAX 105), a Bristol LS6G new to Red & White as its No U554 in May 1954 (but acquired by Silcox from Crosville), was taken near the village of Kilgetty, a few miles north of Tenby, on a lovely spring day in 1973. The car on the right is a Ford Anglia, possibly the 123E model, which was produced between 1962 and 1967, and which had twin chrome side strips, a contrasting coloured roof and side flash, plusher interior trim, an 1198cc engine and a gearbox with synchromesh on first gear.**

of fleet names become a routine practice. Livery has been red and cream since the beginning, with black wings and other embellishments. Fleet numbers were only carried on the vehicles during the 1950s and 1960s, usually simple white or cream numerals painted on the red areas near the cab door or under the windscreen.

South Wales Transport Co

The company was registered on 10 February 1914 to provide bus services to connect tramway services run by the Swansea Improvements & Tramways Company to Llanelli, Port Talbot, Briton Ferry, Gorseinon and the Swansea Valley. The Swansea & District Transport Act of 1936 provided for the withdrawal of the trams and replacement by buses, and this took place between March and June 1937.

A number of independent operators were taken over during the period 1933 to 1938; one interesting acquisition in 1952 was Llanelli District Traction, which brought trolleybuses into the South Wales fleet, but these were withdrawn later in the same year. In 1953 the Swansea Improvements & Tramways Company was acquired and six years later the Mumbles Railway Ltd was purchased; the Swansea to Mumbles railway ran for the last time on 5 January 1960. On 1 September 1962 the business of James of Ammanford was merged with South Wales, and this added a number of modern Leyland buses to a wholly AEC fleet.

Below: **A large number of Weymann-bodied AEC Regent IIIs were purchased by South Wales in 1949, and seen in Swansea in February 1962 is one of these, No 373 (FWN 373). Morsmith's car showrooms sold Land Rovers and Jaguar, Triumph and Standard cars. This building was later occupied by Cobb's, then Pizza Express.**

Above: This excellent 1964 view was taken in Llanelli, and shows one of the batch of 11 Weymann-bodied AEC Regent IIIs ordered by Llanelli District Traction, but delivered direct to South Wales. They became Nos 414 to 424 in the South Wales fleet, and heading for Pwll is No 424 (HWN 847). The single-decker on the right, (LTH 420), was operated by West Wales Motors of Tycroes near Ammanford and is a Burlingham-bodied Guy. This photograph was taken at Llanelli railway station (then commonly spelled 'Llanelly', as this predated moves to regenerate Welsh-language spellings) on a Sunday afternoon in late August or early September 1964. A Summer 1964 SWT timetable shows that West Wales operated service 124, Llanelli to Ammanford, jointly with South Wales Transport and Western Welsh. One bus from each operator performed a 3-hour round trip, maintaining a generally hourly weekday service, with SWT introducing a second bus at peak times. However, SWT was not involved on Sundays and a roughly 2-hourly frequency was provided on that day by two buses, one from each of the other two companies. West Wales operated a 3.35pm timing from Llanelli on Sundays. The SWT local service to Pwll departed from Llanelli station at 00 and 30 minutes past each hour, so it is reasonable to speculate that (HWN 847) is working the 3.30pm journey.

Above: **This is Swansea in February 1962, and South Wales No 1125 (GCY 525) is about to depart for Neath. South Wales took delivery of 23 of these AEC Regent IIIs with Weymann low-height bodywork in 1952. The cars in the background are an Austin A35 and a Ford Prefect Squire. The partially obscured van on the left of the photograph is a Morris LD Series van, which was produced between 1952 and 1968. They were also sold as Austin 1 and 1½ ton vans.**

Above: **During 1953 South Wales received 15 Weymann low-height-bodied AEC Regent IIIs, Nos 1159 to 1173 (HWN 895 to 909), and representing that batch in this early 1962 view is No 1170 (HWN 906). The bus in the background is a Weymann low-height-bodied Leyland PDR1/1 belonging to Western Welsh, No 305 (TUH 305). These were the first rear-engined buses for this operator and arrived during January and February 1960. I would be interested to find out about 'Our Boys' sparkling drinks! The Austin A35 van behind No 1170 is looking very smart.**

Opposite top: **On 1 May 1958 26 Weymann-bodied AEC Regent Vs entered service. Of these, six were unpainted, and in Swansea in February 1962 is one of these, No 516 (RCY 358) — carrying an interesting advert for an unpainted bus! The bus disappearing to the right of the photograph belongs to James of Ammanford, which merged with South Wales later that year.**

Right: **Seen in Port Talbot in May 1973 is No 246 (SWN 986), a 1959 Park Royal-bodied AEC Reliance. The batch, delivered during June and July 1959, totalled ten vehicles, numbered 809 to 818.**

Above: **South Wales was one of the first operators of the AEC Bridgemaster, with four, Nos 1199 to 1202 (RCY 369 to 372), arriving in January 1959. A further batch of five arrived in October 1959. An interesting acquisition in 1960 was No 1213 (60 MMD) a Bridgemaster demonstrator, new in July 1957. The first two batches and the demonstrator were rear-entrance buses, while the remaining Bridgemasters purchased had front entrances. The next batch of Bridgemasters arrived in April and May 1960, and the last purchased by South Wales were Nos 1215 to 1221 (YCY 795 to 801), which arrived between March and April 1961. Looking rather lonely in Swansea in 1964 is No 1220 (YCY 800). Pell's of Newport was a well-known confectioner that used traditional methods and recipes for its sweets; the company has recently amalgamated with Brays Sweets and Sela Confectionery, now known as the Conway Confectionery Group Ltd.**

Below: The AEC Renown was the replacement for the AEC Bridgemaster, and in May 1963 South Wales took delivery of the first production batch, delivered as Nos 1240 to 1253 (303 to 316 ECY) and fitted with Park Royal bodies. Seen in Swansea in May 1973 is the first of the batch, (303 ECY). A further batch of five AEC Renowns, this time with Willowbrook bodies, arrived in November 1963, and these were the last to be acquired by South Wales, as the company returned to purchasing AEC Regent Vs.

Below: **During April and May 1964 the company took delivery of 20 AEC Regent Vs, Nos 587 to 606 (420 to 439 HCY). Of these, nine were bodied by Weymann, six by Willowbrook and five by Park Royal. In Swansea, when brand new, is No 602 (435 HCY), one of the batch bodied by Willowbrook.**

Above: **Neath & Cardiff Luxury Coaches Ltd was a very small BET company whose main activity in the 1960s was the operation of coach services between Cardiff and Swansea via Neath or Briton Ferry bridge. The express coach service licence was surrendered in 1969, to be superseded by a joint limited-stop service between Neath and Cardiff with Western Welsh, and eight N&C coaches were reallocated to the Western Welsh depot in Cardiff. By the end of 1969 the N&C was controlled completely by the management of the South Wales Transport Company. On 5 September 1970 the Cardiff operations of the N&C company were transferred to Western Welsh and in October of that year it was announced that the N&C was to be absorbed into the South Wales Transport Company with effect from 31 December 1970. The final link with the N&C company was severed on 9 January 1971 when the garage at Briton Ferry was closed, ending 40 years of Neath & Cardiff Luxury Coaches. Travelling through Port Talbot in May 1973 is (HTG 182D), a Duple (Northern)-bodied AEC Reliance new to N&C in March 1966.**

Above: Between March and July 1958 both Southern and Western National took delivery of a large batch of Eastern Coachworks-bodied Bristol MW6Gs with coach seating, which were initially allocated to Royal Blue. One of this batch, (XUO 732), is seen in Llanelli during May 1972, after having been sold to South Wales. The coach seats have disappeared, but the roof windows still give this Bristol an elegant look. Just disappearing from view is a Triumph Herald, and behind the Bristol is a Ford Capri.

Thomas Brothers

For many years the long-established South Wales form of Thomas Brothers of Llangadog provided a network of services from Llandeilo, offering links to Carmarthen, Llandovery and Swansea among others.

Above: **Friday is market day in the small town of Llandovery, on the western fringes of the Brecon Beacons, and setting down passengers opposite some of the market stalls on Friday 8 June 1979 is (FBX 474D), a Marshall Leyland Tiger Cub acquired by Thomas from Rees & Williams of Tycroes in 1978. The bus has arrived from Llandeilo, where it made a connection with the West Wales Motors service from Swansea.**

Below: **On the same day, the driver has repositioned (FBX 474D) ready for passengers to board for the next departure back to Llandeilo. On the right is Leyland Leopard (XUF 130), with a Weymann Fanfare body; it was new to Southdown in January 1960 with fleet number 1130, and was acquired by Thomas in November 1973. It has just arrived in Llandovery on one of the market day routes (the 11.30 from Llanfair-ar-y-Bryn), and will later work the Friday return journey to Cilycwm and Rhandirmwyn, small villages only otherwise served by a Post Bus. In recent years these very central bus stops have been moved to a new terminus nearby in the car park below Llandovery Castle.**

Above: **Alexanders Midland took delivery of a large batch of Alexander coach-bodied Leyland PSUC1/12s between April and June 1963. The first of the batch, (VWG 383), is seen here in service with Thomas Brothers, working a market day service and passing through the village of Llansawel on the 12.00 journey from Llandeilo to Lampeter.**

Tudor Williams

Mr Tudor Williams started a horse wagonette service as early as 1908, and this evolved into a bus and coach operation based in the village of Laugharne, Carmarthenshire, trading as 'Pioneer'. The principal bus service linked the market town of Carmarthen with the seaside village of Pendine, passing through St Clears and Laugharne, and for many years was worked jointly with Western Welsh. Besides the castle, Laugharne has also become famous due to its connection with the Swansea-born Welsh poet and author Dylan Thomas, who came to live there, using a former boathouse with fine views over the Afon Taf estuary as his study. It is now a museum dedicated to the writer.

Below: **This bus, (EAX 645), a Guy Arab II, was delivered new to Red & White in 1942 with Duple utility bodywork. Together with several other utility Guys, Red & White had it rebodied by Bristol Tramways after the war, this Bristol body dating from July/August 1951. Red & White sold the bus in June 1963 and Tudor Williams bought it through a dealer (Woodland of Chepstow) later that same month. This summer 1964 view shows (EAX 645) at the then terminus of the Carmarthen to Pendine route, with the driver reversing the bus down the slipway towards the beach in order to turn. Nowadays, First Cymru Buses continue past the beach and up the hill to turn at the top of Pendine village.**

Above: **Rhossili is a small village on the southwestern tip of the Gower peninsula, and seen here in the village is United Welsh No 388 (136 FCY), a Bristol FS6B new in May 1964. At the time this photograph was taken it was brand new, and may be the topic of conversation between the driver and the gentleman with the hat.**

United Welsh was formed in 1938 to consolidate the activities of a number of small companies of Red & White Services Ltd, which operated in the Swansea area. These companies, such as Gower Vanguard Motors Ltd, Eclipse Saloon Services and the Neath Omnibus Company, had been controlled by Red & White since the late 1920s. The vehicle policy of United Welsh was similar to that of Red & White, with Albion buses being purchased between 1939 and 1942. Further deliveries during the war included Bedford OWBs and Guy Arabs, and just after the war Guy Arabs were ordered. However, in 1947 and 1948 the company returned to purchasing Albions, together with Bedford coaches.

Between 1950 and 1953 a wide range of Leyland chassis arrived, including Tigers, Titans, Royal Tigers and Olympics. In

1950 both Red & White and United Welsh became nationalised, and this led to the purchase of Bristols from 1952; for many years this was the only make of bus purchased. The formation of the National Bus Company in 1969 caused major upheaval in the Swansea area. Neath & Cardiff, Thomas Brothers and United Welsh were absorbed into the South Wales Transport Co on 1 January 1971, the three operators having been under SWT control since 1969 (N&C and Thomas Brothers) and 1970 (United Welsh)

Above: **In 1961 United Welsh received 11 Bristol FSF6Gs, Nos 349 to 359 (143 to 153 ACY). By the time this photograph was taken in May 1972 in Aberavon, 151 ACY had passed to South Wales Transport. To the right of the photograph is a Ford Cortina Mark II. This second incarnation of the Cortina was designed by Roy Haines, and was released in 1966, four years after the original model. The Cortina was Britain's most popular new car in 1967, and more than 1,159,000 Mark IIs were produced between 1966 and 1970.**

West Monmouthshire Omnibus Board (Islwyn)

The first independent operator of buses in the West Monmouthshire valleys was Sirhowy Valley Motor Transport Co Ltd, founded in 1919, whose first route was between Blackwood and New Tredegar. Lewis & James Ltd was formed in 1920, and in June 1921 its Western Valley Services began operations in partnership with Sirhowy. Lewis & James acquired Sirhowy, and in 1933 the company became part of Western Welsh. Bedwelty Urban District Council and Mynyddislwyn Urban District Council both decided that they would like their own bus services, and an Act of Parliament in August 1926 saw the formation of the West Monmouthshire Omnibus Board. The new Board purchased the local routes of Lewis & James, the Griffin Motor Company and the Oakdale to Blackwood route of Valleys Motor Services. The Markham to Bargoed route includes a steep hill between Aberbargoed and Bargoed, and the Board had to buy special buses for it.

Below: **The West Monmouthshire Omnibus Board (or 'West Mon') was a joint operation between two neighbouring local authorities and, even in its full form, the fleet name was still shorthand for the more cumbersome title of Bedwelty and Mynyddislwyn Urban District Councils. Like Gelligaer, the councils did not take their names from a major town (perhaps for historical reasons or perhaps to avoid offending the ones not so chosen), but here the nominated places were two villages even smaller than Gelligaer. This fine view of No 26 (GWO 521), an all-Leyland PD2 new in 1948, was taken in July 1968.**

Opposite top: **At Blackwood in August 1970, working a service to Penllwyn, is West Mon No 14 (203 CWO), the first of two Massey-bodied Leyland PD2/40s that were new in March 1962.** *Geoff Gould*

Opposite bottom: **West Monmouthshire purchased two Leyland PSUC1/1 Tiger Cubs in 1961. They were numbered 2 and 3 (125 and 126 BAX) and had Weymann bodywork; seen in Blackwood in August 1970 is No 3. The Tiger Cub was powered initially by a Leyland O350H 91bhp 5.76-litre diesel engine, a horizontal version of the engine fitted to the Comet 90. It had a newly designed lightweight high straight frame with a vertical radiator set just behind the front axle, and the launch transmission was the same four-speed constant mesh unit that had been used in the Tiger PS1. The initial production model was type PSUC1/1T, with the two-speed axle as standard. Omission of this was a no-cost option, in which case the 'T' suffix was omitted.** *Geoff Gould*

Above: **Two more Leyland Tiger Cubs, this time with PSUC1/11 chassis and Willowbrook bodywork were delivered in August 1964. They were number 1, (AWO 528B) and number 30, (AWO 532B). This is number 30 seen at Bargoed in August 1970. In 1962 the power unit became the 125 bhp 6.75-litre O400H and the type codes were revised, to PSUC1/11, PSUC1/12T and PSUC1/13. These were respectively manual bus, manual coach and pneumocyclic bus versions..** *Geoff Gould*

Above: **During May 1960 West Mon took delivery of this, I think, rather angular Longwell Green-bodied Leyland PD2/40, XWO 473, which was No 24 in the fleet. This view was taken in Blackwood in August 1970.** *Geoff Gould*

Opposite top: **West Mon seemed to use any vacant number for new buses, so that members of the same batch would acquire widely different numbers. A rather mucky No 17 (GWO 351C), a Massey-bodied Leyland PD2/40, new in December 1965, is in Caerphilly, heading for Cardiff in August 1970.** *Geoff Gould*

Right: **West Mon was almost unchanged by local government reorganisation in 1974, becoming Islwyn Borough Transport. More remarkably, it also survived the upheavals following deregulation in 1986, unlike its neighbours Rhymney Valley and Taff-Ely, and in 2009 remains an 'arm's-length' council-owned company, probably the smallest in Britain. Ironically, after further changes to local government in 1996, it is now owned by an enlarged Caerphilly County Borough Council, formed from the merger of Islwyn with Rhymney Valley. Leylands had been regularly purchased by the Board, and in March 1962 two Massey-bodied Leyland PD2/40s arrived. Seen in Pontypridd in March 1973 is No 14, (203 CWO).** *Geoff Gould*

Like Rees & Williams, West Wales of Tycroes also operated double-deckers and shared the Llanelli to Llandeilo and Swansea to Llandeilo routes. Unlike the other two joint operators (South Wales Transport and Rees & Williams), almost all journeys provided by West Wales on the route from Swansea continued beyond Llandeilo to Llandovery. This gave a generally 3-hourly frequency between Llandeilo and Llandovery but, as that section of the journey took about

Above: **Llandeilo, in Carmarthenshire, sits on a hill above the River Tywi, the longest river that flows entirely through Wales. Seen in the town in 1964 is No 47 (700 DTH), a Willowbrook-bodied AEC Renown, new to West Wales in December 1963. Only six Renowns were bodied by Willowbrook, the other five having been delivered to South Wales in November 1963.**

45 minutes, buses had a lengthy wait in Llandovery before it was time to return to Llandeilo to take up their next allocated departure back to Swansea.

Above: **The Guy Arab LUF (Lightweight chassis Under Floor engine), built at Fallings Park, Wolverhampton, was often described as over-engineered. Fitted with the best available engine, the Gardner 6HLW, and having a high-build-quality chassis, it was very expensive and was produced in relatively small numbers. West Wales purchased a very distinctive Burlingham-bodied example, (LTH 420), I think in 1954, and** **this view was taken in Llanelli in the summer of 1964 with the bus about to work the 3.35pm service from Llanelli to Ammanford. Burlingham was taken over by Duple in August 1960, and by the start of the 1963 season the Burlingham name had disappeared and products made at the Blackpool premises were being marketed under the name of Duple (Northern).**

For economy reasons, West Wales terminated its journeys from Swansea at Llandeilo in 1956 and a connecting service to and from Llandovery was introduced by Thomas Brothers, which had a depot on the line of route at Llangadog, a few miles from Llandovery. The timings through to Llandovery were still shown in South Wales Transport timetable books up until about 1977, but the timetable pages made no mention of Thomas Brothers and gave the impression that West Wales buses still worked through to Llandovery. After 1956 West Wales buses continued to show Llandovery as their destination when leaving Swansea, although all pictures I have seen of Thomas Brothers buses operating the return service from Llandovery show Llandeilo as their destination, with no indication of any onward connection to Swansea. Arriving in Llandeilo in May 1972 is (MBX 86H), a Willowbrook dual-purpose-bodied Leyland PSU3/3R, which was new to West Wales in 1969. In the 1970s South Wales Transport renumbered the Swansea to Llandeilo route from 36 to 103, although for a time both Rees & Williams and West Wales continued to use the number 36.

Western Welsh Omnibus Co

The Western Welsh Omnibus Co Ltd was formed by the Directors of the National Electrical Construction Co Ltd (NECC) and the Great Western Railway to continue the business of South Wales Commercial Motors Ltd (SWCM) of Cardiff. SWCM had provided bus services in the Cardiff area since 1920, and the new public company was set up in June 1929 with a head office in Salisbury Square, London EC4. The GWR held 50% of the shares. Western Welsh also managed the NECC subsidiary companies, Western Valleys Motor Services (Lewis & James Ltd) and Eastern Valleys Motor Services (Barrett's Ltd). In January 1931 the NECC group was taken over by the British Electric Traction Co Ltd (BET), which would have influence over the company during the

Above: **The first Leyland Olympic HR entered service with Red & White in 1950. Western Welsh was a keen purchaser of the model, and received 57 between 1951 and 1958, all bodied by Weymann. During 1958 six Olympics were delivered, Nos 485 to 490 (OUH 485 to 490), which were fitted for one-person operation and had dual-purpose seating. Peakes of Pontypool had acquired (OUH 490) by the time this photograph was taken in August 1974.**

next 35 years. The head office of Western Welsh was moved in 1932 to 88 Kingsway, London, and the company joined the British Electric Federation in July 1934. In October 1933 the Lewis & James and Eastern Valley firms were absorbed into Western Welsh, bringing the fleet number to 260.

Above: **The National Bus Company came into operation in January 1969 and Western Welsh became a major part of the NBC in South Wales. In 1971 Rhondda was absorbed as the first part of rationalisation, and closure of several depots and transfer of services followed, particularly in the West Wales area. This included services around Haverfordwest, which were taken over by South Wales. In 1963 Western Welsh received nine Marshall-bodied Leyland PSUC1/1s, Nos 1300 to 1308. Working a South Wales town service in May 1973 is the first of this batch, (300 CUH). In the background are a Ford Capri and an Austin A40**

Farina Mark II, introduced in 1961. The latter had a longer wheelbase to increase the space for passengers in the back seats, and the front grill was redesigned. It had a 37bhp engine but was otherwise similar mechanically to the Mark I. The 948cc engine was replaced in the autumn of 1962 by a larger 1098cc version with an output of 48bhp, and an improved gearbox was fitted at the same time. This version lasted in production through to 1967. The brakes also became fully hydraulic, replacing the semi-cable-operated rear system that the Mark I had inherited from the A35. The lorry is, I think, a Dodge.

A feature of the following few years was the acquisition of many operators, adding services and vehicles, often of a very mixed nature. The largest take-over was in 1935 with the purchase of Thomas White & Co (Cardiff & Barry) Ltd, with more than 70 vehicles, including AEC Regals, Regents and six-wheel Renowns. By the mid-1930s the operating area of the company stretched from Abergavenny in the east to St David's in the west. In the last year of peace the fleet of 487 buses travelled 16 million miles

and carried 41 million passengers. During this period the company also erected new garages at Aberdare, Barry, Cross Keys and Brecon.

During the 1950s new garages were built and bids were made for coach firms in the Cardiff area and stage operators in West Wales, including Ebsworth of Laugharne. In January 1957 the 44-vehicle fleet of Green's Motors of Haverfordwest was acquired. Bids were not always successful, though, for in 1951 the company made an

Above: **During 1966 Western Welsh took delivery of 20 Marshall-bodied Leyland PSUC1/ 12Ts, Nos 1375 to 1394 (HBO 375D to 394D). The first ten had dual-purpose seating, the remainder bus seating. Heading for Cardiff in Bridgend in July 1971 is (HBO 377D), which was fitted with dual-purpose seating.**

abortive offer for the motorbuses of Cardiff Corporation's Transport Department.

By 1960 the fleet total was 700 buses, which covered an annual mileage of 24 million miles and carried 92 million passengers in that year. During the mid-1960s some rationalisation took place, with Rhondda Transport Co Ltd coming under joint management, as well as the Monmouthshire Co-ordination Scheme, where economies were made for both Western Welsh and the neighbouring Red & White Services Ltd. In 1971 Rhondda Transport Co Ltd was absorbed, and the closure of several depots and transfer of services followed, particularly in the West Wales area. From the following year, the Red & White and Jones companies shared joint management with Western Welsh

and the assets of these companies were transferred in January 1978 and January 1981 (Jones).

The Western Welsh vehicle policy followed BET practice with, apart from isolated purchases, the majority of chassis orders being AECs and Leylands. The first livery of Western Welsh was red with white/cream superstructure, continued from South Wales days. Red with the distinctive cream waistband and black mudguards was introduced in 1933, and from 1962 an all-over red was used on service buses, later to be relieved with a white band. The coaches were usually in ivory with red or blue relief.